A REASON *to* BELIEVE

A REASON *to* BELIEVE

LESSONS FROM AN IMPROBABLE LIFE

GOVERNOR DEVAL PATRICK

Broadway
New York

BROADWAY

Published in the United States by Broadway Books,
an imprint of the Crown Publishing Group,
a division of Random House, Inc., New York.
www.crownpublishing.com

BROADWAY BOOKS and the Broadway Books colophon
are trademarks of Random House, Inc.

Library of Congress Cataloging-in-Publication Data
Patrick, Deval.
A reason to believe : lessons from an improbable life /
by Deval Patrick.

1. Patrick, Deval. 2. Governors—Massachusetts—Biography.
3. African American governors—Massachusetts—Biography.
4. Massachusetts—Politics and government—1951–
5. Lawyers—United States—Biography.
6. Chicago (Ill.)—Biography.   I. Title.

F71.22.P37A3 2011
974.4'044092—dc22
[B]
2010021528

ISBN 978-0-7679-3112-0
eISBN 978-0-307-72076-4

Printed in the United States of America

Jacket design by Darren Haggar
Jacket photography by Rick Friedman/Corbis

1 3 5 7 9 10 8 6 4 2

First Edition

To Diane, Sarah, and Katherine—my treasures

CONTENTS

A REASON *to* BELIEVE

Once, when I was fifteen, I had to catch a bus to meet a friend, and I was running late. We lived on the South Side of Chicago, near the corner of 54th Street and Wabash Avenue, so I raced south down Wabash past the white-walled commercial bakery that always smelled of sour yeast, across the weed-filled median on Garfield Boulevard, and east down a block past the liquor store, the Laundromat, and the shop that sold live chickens to housewives. The shopkeeper could slaughter the bird or the women could do it themselves at home.

I reached the bus stop just as the familiar green and white CTA bus pulled up, oily and wheezing. I climbed the steps, reached for my coins, and only then realized that I did not have enough for the fare. The driver, a world-weary black man with a gray grizzle and salt-and-pepper mustache, had already jerked the bus into gear and started down the street. He gave me a withering look and told me gruffly to sit down, pointing to a seat close to the door. I obeyed.

I braced myself for a stern lecture on the futility of trying to pull a fast one, and I assumed he would kick me off at the next stop. My mouth was suddenly dry, my stomach churning. Embarrassed and stammering, I stood again and started to explain that I had been away (I was a sophomore at a boarding school in New England) and did not know the fare had changed. He looked me over with the sure gaze of a man who had heard every excuse and was practiced in sizing up passengers. He turned his eyes back to the road. His expression abruptly softened.

"It's okay," he said. "Just pass it on, son. Pass it on."

I thanked him and sat back down heavily, overwhelmed. Expecting humiliation, I instead received a simple act of grace, and for whatever reason—perhaps just the kindness in the face of certain reprimand—that moment left a lasting impression. It was a reminder that I should do for others what he had done for me.

Nearly forty years later, I can reflect on what a blessing it has been to encounter so many people who chose to help someone in need—not because they had to but because they simply could. They showed mercy or compassion, and through their action taught a lesson. Sometimes these deeds, bold in their scope and lofty in their ambition, create headlines. More often, they are performed anonymously, quietly, reaching no further than the heart they were intended to touch. In whatever form, such acts create their own legacy of hope and inspiration. They pass something on. This book is my effort to share some of the lessons that have imbued me with core values, shaped my identity, and made me want to be a better man.

My life is often described as "improbable." Because I grew up in a broken home and in poverty, my academic career at Harvard College and Harvard Law School is sometimes called "improbable." My legal career, which included winning an argument before the U.S. Supreme Court and suing an Arkansas governor named Bill Clinton, who later appointed me assistant attorney general for civil rights, is called "improbable." My corporate career, which included service as a senior executive at two of the most highly recognized companies in America, Texaco and Coca-Cola, is called "improbable." My political career is described variously as "improbable" or "impossible": In my first race for elective office, lacking name recognition, connections, and money, I became the first African-American governor in the history of Massachusetts.

Of course, I acknowledge the unlikelihood of my good fortune. I also recognize the hard work and discipline that have made it possible. But above all I cherish and celebrate the many people who have taken moments to enlighten me, to renew my ideals, and to spur me to action. There have been teachers and preachers, supervisors and colleagues, friends and family. There have also been strangers, many strangers—whether on a dairy farm in Massachusetts or in the sands of the Nubian Desert—who through their words or deeds have delivered transcendent messages about life, faith, and friendship. I have always tried to listen. And they have made all the difference.

This book is a tribute to them. It is an effort to distill some of the many lessons that have made me the idealist I am and to convey them in a way that is meaningful and lasting. My journey is far from over. There are lessons yet to learn. But my experiences have been rich, giving me a broad window into the lives of others, and I believe these experiences offer a guiding light for other seekers. That's a bold statement, but it's grounded in a truth taught by my "improbable" life: Each of us, from the mightiest to the meekest, has the capacity to teach, inspire, and ennoble.

Pass it on.

Chapter 1

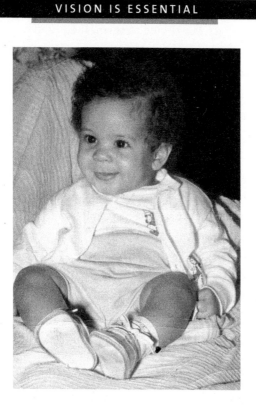

In 1999, in a weekly meeting of the five most senior executives at Texaco, our boss, the chief executive officer, asked whether the company lacked vision. The global energy industry was in the midst of great consolidation, with legendary giants merging and famous brands disappearing. I was a relative newcomer to this world, and it felt like a game of billion-dollar musical chairs played around the circular table of a plush, walnut-paneled conference room. We sensed we were losing, and I was surprised by the muffled response to the boss's question. If there was a vision for the company beyond just making money, no one in that room knew what it was.

The moment resonated with me for a different reason. According to scripture, "Without a vision, the people will perish." I knew that lesson well.

Growing up with no money, I knew my family had a simple vision: to no longer be broke. Though we occasionally lived from hand to mouth, my grandmother hated for us to describe ourselves as poor. "We're broke," she declared. "Broke is temporary." Splitting rhetorical hairs seemed odd when we were hungry. But my grandmother's message conveyed a much larger truth, especially in that place and in those times. She taught us to imagine a life that was better than or different from our own and then to work for it.

The South Side of Chicago was like a small southern town in the 1950s and '60s. Many of the inhabitants were recent arrivals from "down home," as they called it—the cotton fields of Mississippi and Georgia, the tobacco fields of the Carolinas, or the railroad yards of Arkansas and Louisiana.

People spoke like southerners, with a lyrical quality to their speech. Subjects and verbs rarely agreed, and sentences had the rhythm and pace of the South. Everyone communicated by telling stories, often allegorical, never hurried. The old folks quoted scripture freely and from memory. My grandma Sally's favorite was the Ninety-first Psalm, which she summoned when she was stressed: *"For he shall give his angels charge over thee, to keep thee in all thy ways. They shall bear thee up in their hands, lest thou dash thy foot against a stone."* The elderly also carried themselves with a courtliness that belied their lack of formal education and proper English. You were expected to greet others on the street with "good morning" or "good afternoon." Kids addressed adults as "sir" or "ma'am."

Scowling down on us were the infamous Robert Taylor Homes, a miles-long stretch of identical seventeen-story "projects," which would become synonymous with the public housing woes of urban America. But most people I knew lived in two- and three-story tenements, with an apartment or two on each floor. There was block after block of these squat, solid-looking brick or frame buildings, with rickety railings, chipped concrete steps, and porches whose boards needed replacing. Clotheslines were strung across postage-stamp backyards or connected to back porches from separate buildings. A few families kept chickens in a backyard coop for eggs and meat. The front stoops, with their folding lawn chairs, drew neighbors outside on summer evenings. Churches and schools provided stability.

The stockyards, where cattle and pigs were brought from the Great Plains for slaughter, were a short bus ride away. You could smell the stench in our neighborhood when the wind was right. In the summer, a horse-drawn wagon cruised our streets, the fresh fruit arrayed on a bed of hay and the driver yodeling "Watermelons!" to attract his customers. On those same roads limped a menacing man with a misaligned eye who pushed a crude wooden cart on bicycle tires, offering to sharpen knives on a stone that screeched when it spun.

Much of life seemed to center on food—getting it, preparing it, doing without it. Tiny, makeshift gardens miraculously yielded collard greens, tomatoes, and pole beans. Great pots of greens with ham hocks or fatback simmered all day long on small apartment ranges. Black cast-iron skillets sizzled with porgies or fish that were caught in Lake Michigan or even the Washington Park lagoons, gutted and scaled, rolled in cornmeal, and fried in bacon fat, the latter rendered from many a breakfast and kept in an old coffee can on the stove. Cornbread, easy, cheap, and filling, was served with everything. Whatever was for dinner, it was considered bad form not to offer something to a neighborhood kid who was hungry. And in that neighborhood, someone was always hungry. The smells were full of flavor and anticipation with one outstanding exception. When someone was cooking chitterlings—pig intestines stewed for hours in broth—the stink drove out all bystanders.

My earliest impressions of my parents were of a stern father who always seemed to be observing us critically, and from a distance, and a brooding mother who would lie in bed for hours, smoking silently and staring off in dark, deep thought. They seemed to have negotiated their way into their marriage. In an exchange of letters within days in 1954, they communicated both a hunger for and skepticism about each other and their future. He wrote: "If your choice matches mine, we match. I can show you but don't intend to make you see it if you don't want to. On the other hand, if you do agree, you've got a mate."

She replied, "I have a great affection for you, and feel we could make it together. I hope and will do the best I can not to be selfish as far as this is concerned. I want to give as much to you as you have given to me."

My father, Pat, was a jazz musician, and as this letter suggests, he seemed to have a take-it-or-leave-it attitude about their relationship. It would be on his terms, period. His greatest and first love was music. My mother, Emily, appears to have felt chronically misunderstood and responded favorably to his insights about her. An ardent romance it wasn't.

But they tied the knot, and soon afterward, in August 1955, my sister, Rhonda, was born. I followed a short eleven months later, in July 1956. When I was born, the four of us lived in a basement apartment at 79th and Calumet, and there's a favorite family photograph of me sitting on my father's shoulders outside that apartment when I was two or three years old. I have vague recollections of living there, of being bounced around by my father in that apartment. I have a vivid memory of him pouring milk on my sister's head at the kitchen table one night when he got upset with her. I thought it funny at the time.

Any sense I had of contented family life came to a jarring end when my father decided to leave and move to New York when I was four. I knew nothing of the tensions. My mother, who had dropped out of high school to pursue him, hoped he would return, a hope she nourished by sending him letters regularly. "We all love you very much, and are trying to understand you," she wrote. "Try and do the same for us." When Chubby Checker became a sensation, she wrote, "The kids have gotten so they twist on everything; every kind of beat." She would include little notes from us in her letters. Rhonda's penmanship was remarkably clear at age five or six. Mine was horrible.

My father sent some money once or twice a year, and the landlord was kind about waiving the rent for months at a time. But our finances went from tenuous to desperate, and we had to move. We were offered an apartment in the new Robert Taylor Homes, but my mother could not bring herself to live there, still hoping, I think, for her husband's return.

There would be no reconciliation. My mother tried to make it on her own for a few years, mostly with the help of welfare, but feeling lonesome and needing help, she moved us into her parents' apartment on Wabash Avenue. Since we spent so much time there anyway and I adored my Gram and Poppy, I thought this was a great idea. Little did I know that for my mother it was a sign of defeat, and that my grandmother made her feel like it was for many years.

The tenement that we lived in with my grandparents consisted of four apartments on two levels with two separate entrances. The apartments were identical, long and narrow. Ours was on the first floor. The door from the small, tiled vestibule opened on a dark, narrow hall. To the right, with a window on Wabash Avenue, was the living room with a gold upholstered sofa with clear plastic slip-covers, a dark green leatherette recliner, and a light brown stuffed chair, also covered in plastic, facing the television. That television, with its oversized cabinet and small screen, seems to have always been on and at full volume, whether for Gram's soaps (her "stories") during the day or the network news in the evening. It took a long time to warm up, so we had to plan ahead if there was something we didn't want to miss. The firehouse across the street had two trucks with an uncanny ability to roar off, sirens wailing, just at the punch line of a favorite sitcom.

Next down the hall was my grandparents' room, small and orderly, with twin beds, a matching dresser and chest in walnut veneer, and a large radiator painted white with a tin pan or kettle on top to generate a little humidity in winter. I was born in this room, in my grandmother's bed. She and my uncle Sonny assisted. There was no doctor; labor was brief. According to family legend, after Uncle Sonny cut and tied off the umbilical cord, Grandma wrapped me in a blanket and placed me in the warm oven with the door open until the doctor arrived. Grandma told this story every Thanksgiving when she was dressing the holiday turkey in the very same roasting pan that once held me.

My mother and sister and I occupied a smaller bedroom across from the one bathroom. It was furnished with bunk beds that took up most of the space. For a time we could double up, but eventually we had to rotate so that one of us would sleep on the floor. Whoever's turn it was for "floor night" followed a ritual: you would lay down newspapers, then a thin blanket, then a sheet, then a threadbare cover. Part of the morning ritual was to disassemble all of this and stack it neatly under the bed. The room's one window opened onto an air shaft and the neighbors' window fifteen feet across.

At the end of the hall was a dining room, off of which was a small, rude kitchen with one bare lightbulb that dangled from the ceiling on a frayed cord. At the end of the cord, just above the bulb, was the kitchen's one socket, where Grandma plugged her electric mixer or iron, depending on the chore at hand. It could make running in from the back door hazardous.

We didn't know to complain. It was home. The notion of having more than one bathroom or multiple sockets in the kitchen or a window with a view was not something I thought much about. We were better off than many. What we had was always orderly, even if our lives were not, as if making hospital corners on the beds each morning would keep the economic chaos at bay.

If we had been tempted by pity, my grandparents would not have allowed it. They came to Chicago from Louisville, Kentucky, in the 1930s, driven by ordinary middle-class aspirations for themselves and the family they hoped for. Their vision was simple and clear, and it helped shape my own. But, though they shared a vision for their lives, God could not have matched two more different personalities.

Sally Embers Wintersmith both embodied and defied the stereotypical grandmother. Grandma—or "Gram," as we called her—baked cakes every Saturday morning, saving the beaters and bowls to be licked by the grandkids, and made every holiday and birthday an occasion. She could jump rope with Rhonda and her friends and read to me in ways that would make stories come to life. She also cursed so stridently and with such creativity that she would have felt at home in any barracks or locker room. The daughter of an Irish landowner and his black "charwoman," she had bright red hair and hazel eyes and was light-skinned enough to "pass," as the old folks used to say. When she and my grandfather would drive through the Jim Crow South, she would go into the diner first, get a table, order for herself and the family, and then call everyone in once the food was served. The proprietor was less likely to refuse them at that point, but the ploy didn't always work. One time, a waitress said she would have to serve my grandmother and her family in the kitchen. Gram drew herself up, looked her square in the eye, and said, "We don't eat in the kitchen in our own home." She walked out with her family in tow, leaving the food untouched on the table.

Grandma helped manage our tenement for the non-resident owner, which defrayed the cost of the apartment. She would, among other things, collect the rent, arrange for repairs, and keep track of coal deliveries for the basement furnace. She collected the gossip as well, a job that occupied a good deal of her time.

As talkative as Grandma was, my grandfather was nearly as taciturn. Reynolds Brown Wintersmith, whom we called "Poppy," was strong, slightly bent, and balding, not quite six feet tall. My grandmother adoringly said that in his youth, he was "built like a Roman soldier." He wore a faint perpetual smile and had a twinkle in his warm brown eyes, but he rarely spoke directly to me or other family members beyond simple pleasantries. He had a delightful way of humming, though—indistinct tunes of his own composition, which seemed to keep trouble at bay.

Poppy's work ethic kept us more stable than most. He was a janitor at the South Shore Bank at 71st and Jeffrey for more than fifty years. When he wasn't sweeping the floors, he drove the executives. When he wasn't driving the executives, he did odd jobs for their families or cleaned the nearby Laundromat. He was always pleasant, respectful, and dignified. At the bank, he was beloved by everyone from the tellers to the chief executive. At his memorial service, the bank president said that had my grandfather lived in a different time, he would have retired as the bank's CEO.

Poppy put others at ease and was a good example of how to get along in the world. But in my youth, he remained somewhat impenetrable. When I helped him shovel coal and scrape out the clinkers from the coal furnace at home, he would say nothing save the barest instructions. I helped mop the floors of the Laundromats, but all he told me was what to do and what not to do. On the drives to and from those jobs, only his humming would break the silence.

Only on rare occasions would emotion break through his stoicism. After President John F. Kennedy was killed in 1963, when the Chicago schools closed out of respect, I watched the black-and-white broadcast of the national grieving and absorbed those powerful images: the flag-draped coffin on the caisson, the young widow in a black veil with her two small children, the riderless horse with the boots facing backward in the stirrups. The procession seemed to move in slow motion. All was quiet save the *clippity-clop* of the hoofs against the pavement. In our living room, no one spoke. When I looked back from my seat on the floor, I saw my grandfather riveted by the images and crying silently. I realized then that being a strong man does not preclude showing emotion. I was seven years old.

Gram and Poppy wanted us to see more than the South Side. They took us on road trips to Michigan, where we picked apples and brought them home in big baskets for pies, applesauce, and fried apples at Sunday breakfast. One weekend each month, while my great-grandparents were still alive, we made the long drive to Louisville to visit my family. My grandmother would pack a lunch of fried chicken or juicy hamburgers, cooked rare early in the morning, then wrapped tightly in aluminum foil to finish cooking until lunchtime. We would set off just before sunrise in Poppy's Buick, the smell of lunch so intoxicating that we would beg for it until we were fed around eleven.

While I thought those trips were exposing me to a much wider world, I now realize how blissfully unaware I was. We would attend the Kentucky Derby every year and watch from the infield. I had no idea that black folks weren't allowed in the stands; I just assumed Gram and Poppy thought the infield was better. I never really thought about why we stopped to pee at the side of the road instead of at a restaurant or motel or why there was so much anxiety over where we'd stop to eat or why we filled coolers or shoeboxes with food for the trip. Only later did I recognize that my grandparents wanted to avoid exposing us to the harsh realities of Jim Crow, to travel safely, and to broaden our horizon. They did not want me trapped by bitterness but liberated to believe that the wider world could be a special place.

My expectations—my sense of the possible—also expanded while visiting my father in New York. One summer in the early 1960s, I took my first train ride with my mother and Rhonda to see him. He had a tiny studio apartment in Lower Manhattan, and we all crowded in with him. We toured the sights, including a Circle Line boat trip and a memorable visit to the top of the Empire State Building, soured only when my father lifted me to see the view and accidentally speared my head on the sharp railing. On the train ride home, my mother had enough money for only one breakfast in the dining car, so the three of us shared a plate of pancakes. I thought it was elegant. In 1964, Rhonda and I flew alone to visit our father during the New York World's Fair, where he performed with the Babatunde Olatunji band at the African Pavilion. We met the people, listened to the music, watched the dances, and ate food from all around Africa. We also spent a good deal of time wandering through the rest of the Fair, imagining ourselves in other parts of the world. I wanted it.

Those experiences often made my home life feel claustrophobic. In addition to my immediate family, my grandparents also accommodated Uncle Sonny and his daughter, Renae, as well as other short-term boarders. The environment was perpetually tense, with Uncle Sonny often serving as the flashpoint. He was older than my mother, a handsome, charming, but irresponsible character addicted to heroin who careened between drug binges, jail, and his parents' apartment. Renae's mother was also an addict.

Uncle Sonny was also Gram's favorite, which embittered my mother even more. When I was about nine, Grandma and Poppy were away on a trip, and I walked in on Uncle Sonny shooting up in the living room. I went back to the kitchen and asked my mother what he was doing, and she flew into a rage. She put him out, double-locking the door, which produced a long night of his pounding on the door and shouting to be let back in while we huddled silently and sleeplessly in our room. For that understandable act of motherly protection, my mother caught unholy hell from Gram when she returned. "This is *his* home," she screamed.

I was frightened that night. It was unnerving to hear Uncle Sonny threatening us from just the other side of the door and embarrassing to think the neighbors were also hearing it. Everyone knew about Sonny's transgressions but mostly looked the other way. His addiction was never discussed in front of Rhonda and me. My mother was her usual remote, calm self that night, hardly saying a word, smoking in bed, as if it were perfectly natural to have a grown man hammering away on the door and shouting threats and obscenities for hours in the middle of the night. I was confused, but no one offered a word of explanation to Rhonda and me.

Gram was quite open about her belief that mothers prefer sons, and she never wavered in her unapologetic preference for Uncle Sonny. That slight was indefensible, and my mother never forgave it. While Sonny routinely stole from his own parents and could not provide for his children, my mother stuck by her kids, worked to improve herself, and provided. She was a clerk at a local dry cleaner's while taking night classes at Dunbar High for her GED. Eventually she landed a job at the downtown post office, joined the union, and got benefits. We took a trip to the downtown Sears on State Street once a year for new school clothes and tried to make them last all year long, even through our growth spurts. We had to change into play clothes every day after school to prolong the life of the school gear. Except on Sunday mornings, holidays, and special occasions, when Gram took charge of us all, my mother was expected to provide our meals. They were plain and functional, food as fuel. I did not know that peas were green until I was an adult. I thought they were gray.

I never heard Gram complain about our being there, but her frustrations were evident. Always careful with money, she tried to maintain two separate economies in the household—my mother was responsible for us, Poppy was responsible for her. Gram would buy one small can of frozen orange juice concentrate every week and apportion one tiny glass for Poppy, and only Poppy, to have with his breakfast. She kept his juice on a shelf in the Frigidaire that was dedicated exclusively to my grandparents. On hot summer days, that juice, with all the sweet pulp floating around in it, would absolutely call to us. I used to wonder what possible difference it would make to take a single sip. Who would notice? Well, Gram noticed, and would let me have it—especially on those occasions when one sip would lead to more.

(Years later, my wife, Diane, could not figure out why I bought gallons of orange juice at a time, even though we were at no risk of running out and I had lost interest in drinking it.)

The little stresses in our house or in our lives never seemed to bother Rhonda. She was enviably at ease at home or in the neighborhood. Though she looked awkward as a girl, skinny and all elbows with crooked front teeth, she was sociable and had many friends with whom she spent hours. She was in and out of their houses, jumped double Dutch with the best of them, knew all the latest dance steps, and kept up with the kids' gossip. Although we were close when we were small, we were openly contemptuous of each other as adolescents. Having raised children of my own, I now know this was a natural phase, but as teens Sonny justifiably referred to us as "the battling Patricks." I was a total nuisance when boys started to enter my sister's picture, taunting them and generally being a pain. Rhonda endured me as patiently as she could while her suitors were around, then let me have it when they left. Other confrontations were mostly spawned by my jealousy. Though I was regarded in school and at home as more studious and responsible, my sister had a comfort with herself and her peers that I craved.

Like everyone else, I was taunted by the neighborhood bully, Richard, an uncommonly violent youth; one time, he wedged a piece of glass in an empty soda can and hurled it down from a second-floor porch at my head. It hit its mark, opening a wound that sent blood gushing and leaving a scar that I carry to this day. He was a part of the same gang that stole my bike from me—while I was riding it. I had a few buddies with whom I played stickball or capture the flag or chased lightning bugs in the summer. But I was mostly a loner and spent countless hours by myself under the back steps, playing in the dirt with my little toy soldiers, creating imaginary battles, riding to the rescue, and vanquishing enemies. Later, I would huddle for hours with the real estate section of the Sunday newspaper, studying the floor plans of model homes and imagining myself and my life in them. I never missed an episode of *Roy Rogers*.

For much of the 1960s, the South Side felt rather insulated. Except for our occasional family trips or the annual journey to Sears for school clothes, we lived, worked, went to school, played, and shopped on the South Side. We didn't think of it as segregation, just the neighborhood. We were trying to live middle-class lives in hopes of making it into the middle class ourselves one day, and we spent precious little time resenting wealth or white people. We had a vision for where we wanted to go, if no real path on which to get there. The focus in our home seemed to be inordinately on table manners, respectfulness, and homework—not poverty, deprivation, or social justice.

But by the late 1960s, the barriers against the outside world had begun to come down. The civil rights movement had grown from nonviolent protests to increasing militancy. Opposition to the Vietnam War had escalated, and riots had afflicted urban areas from California to New Jersey. In 1968, after the assassinations of Martin Luther King Jr. and Robert F. Kennedy, the riots finally swept through our neighborhood. Stores were looted. Gangs organized and attacked innocent bystanders. Gunshots became regular background noise. In only a couple of years, our transplanted southern enclave, with its indigenous economy, neighbors who watched over the children, and institutions that craved order, turned into a wasteland of charred buildings and restlessness.

Things were most dangerous during the hot summers, so my mother decided that Rhonda and I should be away as much as possible. When I was twelve, she decided that we would attend Bible camp in Michigan. We would be away for two weeks, sleeping in a bunk with kids from other churches around Chicago.

My sister and I were horrified. We were regular but reluctant churchgoers on orders from our grandmother, but religious camp was going too far. No one else from the neighborhood was going, and we would be out of step with the other kids when we got home. And it was to be our first sustained experience with white people. To us they sounded odd. They were mostly harmless, even amusing, as long as they kept their distance, but they could be dangerous if they got too close. These truths we learned from television, which showed Lucille Ball's endearing hijinks but also Bull Connor's high-powered fire hoses used against defenseless blacks.

When the day came to leave for Camp Beechpoint, we boarded the bus with all the other kids and set off. We tried not to reveal our apprehension, but we failed. We were hopelessly conscious of being out of place, and it showed. For instance, most of the white kids had duffel bags and backpacks suitable for the rugged outdoors, but we showed up with plastic, hard-sided luggage and steamer trunks, as if we were about to embark on the Grand Tour of Europe. The bus was quiet much of the way, and the ride seemed to take hours. I suspect most of the new campers were nervous as well, but at the time we were sure it was only us. One thing was for certain: There would be no bickering between Rhonda and me. We had to look out for each other.

When we arrived, we met the counselors and were shown to our cabins. They were simple wooden boxes on stone footings. Each had six or seven sets of bunks and a small common bathroom with walls so thin, there were no secrets. In the early days, the new kids were more modest and tried to urinate silently, along the inside of the bowl, to be less obvious. Most of us had never even undressed in front of someone outside our families. The woods were spooky and exceptionally dark at night. The swimming test was a particular source of anxiety for the black campers; for many of us, contact with the water consisted of splashing in the public wading pool or running through an open fire hydrant.

We prayed all the time: grace before meals and a blessing afterward; chapel after breakfast and before dinner. Sunday was a hallelujah marathon. We sang hymns around the campfire at night and at bedtime before lights out. Even our arts and crafts projects had Christian themes. The black kids prayed especially hard before the swimming test.

To this day, it amazes me that the organizers were able to blend two often volatile ingredients—race and religion—and make it work. They succeeded by making it less about issues and dogma and more about people. By the end of the two weeks, no one wanted to leave. We sang camp songs and hymns together on the ride back to Chicago and cried when we had to say good-bye at the bus stop, the parents looking on with amazement. Rhonda and I had also found an experience in common all our own. By the following summer, we couldn't wait to go back.

I was most appreciative of the woman who prepared

our fine meals. She was from Maywood, Illinois, the first African American I ever met who owned a home in a suburb. She had two daughters at the camp, one of whom became a great friend of Rhonda's, and over the years, we visited them often in their tidy community. In her ease with whites and blacks alike, her educated diction, and her confident bearing, she seemed to confirm what my grandparents had been trying to envision for us all along: A secure middle class was within our reach.

My grandparents and my mother were physically close but emotionally distant. They always had my best interests at heart, but their affections were circumscribed and conditional, preoccupied as they were by their own struggles and demons. What I craved most, consistent love and encouragement, I got from teachers.

The Mary Church Terrell School was on State Street, part of the Robert Taylor Homes complex just a block behind my grandparents' apartment. I started first grade in 1962 and attended straight through the sixth grade. All my teachers were self-confident professionals, and they embodied a very different vision. What they had—college diplomas, steady jobs, well-built homes, stable families—was what I too hoped to have someday. They spoke proper English and wore clothes that fit. And they looked like me.

I was attentive and eager, diligently completing what

little homework I was given. School came easily to me, and I developed a reputation as a good student. Rhonda, a year ahead of me, came to resent that teachers started asking if she were my sister. It was supposed to be the other way around.

In the early grades, I would hug my teachers hello and good-bye. I sought their attention unabashedly and usually got it, though it wasn't always positive. In the third grade, I was well ahead of my classmates, and the teacher, Mrs. Threet, gave me special library privileges. I could skip certain classroom lessons and read or do homework in the library. I once came back to class in the middle of a lesson with a picture book on horses. Another student indiscreetly started asking me questions about it while Mrs. Threet was speaking.

"Excuse me, Mr. Patrick," she said. "I think it's time for you to settle down."

I told her I hadn't said a word.

"Well," she said to the class, "it seems that Mr. Patrick is getting a little too big for his britches."

I was devastated, though I did learn how exposed you are by privilege. (I loved her anyway.)

My grade school teachers did what all great teachers do—expand your mind, your vision, and your world—and none more so than Eddie Quaintance, my sixth-grade instructor. She was tall, milk-chocolate brown, and supremely confident. In her early thirties, she epitomized maturity and experience. She was pretty, in the way a person who is self-composed always seems attractive. Our class was large, maybe thirty kids, but she brooked no nonsense. She was firm and had a reputation for being the toughest grader—and disciplinarian—at Terrell. Rhonda confirmed some of those rumors before I got to the class, having been in her class the year before. We were all a little afraid of her.

Hormones start to bubble in sixth-graders, and acting out was the custom for many students anyway, so quite a few teachers seemed to spend most of their time just keeping order. Not Mrs. Quaintance. Her presence alone commanded order. She could cut you a look that made you shrink from whatever tomfoolery you were up to or considering. If that were not enough, she had a wooden paddle, inscribed with the words *Board of Education*, and a storage room nearby where she confidently applied the paddle to an errant student's backside. Our ill-fitting clothes, our runny noses, and our broken homes were no excuse. She was all about learning, which for her was more than facts and figures. It was about imagination.

Mrs. Quaintance made me aspire to live as a citizen of the world. She had traveled to Germany to visit her son, who was working there, and she taught us all to count and greet one another in German. She took us to see *The Sound of Music* and used it both to enchant us and to teach us about the rise of the Nazis in Europe. She took us on another trip to the Chicago Lyric Opera; I had no idea what they were singing about, but I was completely enthralled with the music and pageantry and remain so today. She made achievement and urbanity seem natural for us poor, black South Siders. It was a gift I still cherish.

That year, I entered a regional essay writing contest on "Father of the Year." I wrote about Gram—and won. I wrote a similar essay about Poppy. I now realize that I wrote to gain the attention and approval of the adults who were most remote, yet most important, in my life.

From Terrell, we went to middle school at DuSable Upper Grade Center. The classes were in DuSable High School—a mammoth, grimy, brick and limestone building that seemed to have mile-long hallways. (I now know they were just average for a large urban high school.) By the late 1960s, the Blackstone Rangers and the Disciples, two rival gangs, were growing and competing. Part of their initiation seemed to involve assaulting the young, well-intentioned white teachers at DuSable, like the math instructor who was whacked in the head by a bat-wielding, would-be gangbanger.

Indeed, the tumult that had swept through the neighborhood had taken root in my school. Nearly forty kids filled every class, and the teacher's job was primarily to maintain order. Police hovered at every intersection in the hallways, and bicycle chains secured the outside doors. To go from one building to the other during class, you had to slip a pass under the door so the officer on duty could slide the chains off. Many of the glass windows had been shattered by the riots and replaced by Plexiglas or plywood.

Going to DuSable involved a longer walk from home, and the gangs made those walks treacherous. I was routinely "jumped," my lunch money or school supplies stolen, mostly because I was a "good" kid. I was also at risk for not being black enough, a mark of authenticity conferred on those with the darkest skin. Color consciousness among black people is an ancient issue, but after Dr. King's death, the militancy in some black circles only intensified the intolerance toward African Americans who were comparatively fair. I was meek, bookish, bashful, and, in some people's view, "high yellow"—thus an easy mark. It only added to the uncomfortable self-consciousness that I carried around anyway. I just wanted to be in step and left alone. Surely there was some place where skin color was not the center of everything.

Though getting to DuSable and home again was hazardous, the school, like Terrell before it, was a refuge. There, in the seventh grade, I met another teacher who would radically broaden my vision of what was possible. Darla Weissenberg was a twenty-two-year-old idealist who was committed to improving the world and making sure those of us on the South Side had a place in it. She was also my first white teacher. I didn't know it at the time, but she had attended schools with black children in Rockford, Illinois, and had been deeply influenced by a sixth-grade African-American teacher who had told her students about the indignities of growing up in segregated Baltimore. So when Mrs. Weissenberg received her teaching certificate and was initially assigned to a white high school, she requested the inner city and landed at DuSable.

She was in only her second year of teaching when I had her for Language Arts and Social Studies. The students were discovering how easily they could intimidate whites, and they badgered her on a regular basis. In the confines of so much free-floating hate, she was very brave to come to DuSable every day with such compassion and commitment.

Hers was my favorite class, and I opened up to her in my writing assignments. In an essay grandly titled "The Story of My Life," in which we were asked to describe our short lives to date and also our future, I recounted my rather harrowing birth and boasted of my academic and extracurricular achievements. I then envisioned a future for myself that was far removed from DuSable and the South Side. "Thinking about my life, from being born in the morning, to almost death, to outstanding student, I think about my life 10 years from now. I should be out of UCLA and in to real estate with a home and a family. I thank God that He has thought enough of me to take me this far." I had a clear notion of what middle-class direction I wanted to take— though Lord knows where the UCLA came from!

My aspirations and interests caught the attention of Mrs. Weissenberg. Middle-class ambitions were not what she had come to expect from DuSable students. The following year, she noticed—either on a bulletin board or in a teacher's journal—a message about a foundation called A

Better Chance. Its mission was to identify kids from non-traditional prep school backgrounds, as the euphemism of the day went, for placement in Eastern prep schools. She thought about me and asked to meet my mother.

I was by then in eighth grade, the last year of junior high, which meant there were choices to be made about high school. In those days, students had three: I could go to a vocational school, a technical school, or the high school in my district. None of these options was very good.

Vocational school was the least appealing because, at that time, it did not have a college track. Though no one in my family had gone beyond the eleventh grade, I was determined to go to college, and I was blessed beyond measure to live in a household where no one discouraged that notion. So, while vocational schools taught things I now wish I knew—like auto mechanics and tailoring—that option was not for me.

The technical school made more sense because it taught mechanical drawing, and at the time I wanted to be an architect. My drum teacher, a family friend, was both a timpanist with the Chicago Symphony and an architect, the first black professional I can remember who was not a teacher. He had given me a three-edged ruler so I could draw room layouts and buildings to scale, and I spent hours with the Sunday newspaper real estate section evaluating designs and creating my own. The city had only two technical schools, with the far better one on the North Side. Though I was graduating first in my class at DuSable, our guidance counselor could not persuade the North Side school to take a South Side student. The North Side was for white, middle-class people. The South Side was for us.

That left DuSable High, which would mean returning to the very environment I was trying to leave. Knowing what I faced, my mother and I met with Mrs. Weissenberg about A Better Chance. We applied, and I was accepted, sight unseen, by Milton Academy in Massachusetts. I was apprehensive, of course. My mother was wary but fatalistic. "You can always come home," she said.

I am hardly the only product of Chicago's South Side to have gone on to better things or the only kid from a hardscrabble background to have had a measure of success. That "rags to riches" story is distinctly American, and though it is not told often enough, it is still told more often in this country than anywhere else on earth. In my own case, I knew that my circumstances, however difficult, need not be permanent; I could shape my own destiny. That was the true gift of my childhood. The *power* of that gift is that I was surrounded by adults who had every reason to curb my dreams. My grandparents had grown up with Jim Crow. My mother knew all too well the humiliation of poverty and betrayal. Mrs. Threet, Mrs. Quaintance, and Mrs. Weissenberg knew the constraints of Chicago's public schools. Yet in different ways, they all taught me to reject the cycle of despair that had trapped so many others and to pursue opportunities that I could barely imagine. It was as if they had been schooled in that famous admonition of the late great president of Morehouse College, Dr. Benjamin E. Mays, who said, "Not failure, but low aim, is sin."

Gram tended to roses in a little garden right behind our tenement. Early in the morning, when the weather was warm, she would go into our backyard, pick up the trash that had blown in, brush away any broken glass, and work that soil. Believe me, that soil had things in it that God would never put in dirt.

But she brought forth her roses. With one cutting she had brought north from my great-grandfather's house in Kentucky, she grew a climber that reached nearly all the way up the side of our two-story building. It was magnificent. And it was improbable. In that place, in that soil, it defied all reason and expectation. Still, Gram believed.

The adults in my early life, in the teeth of their struggles and setbacks, believed in me as well. Just as Texaco needed a vision many years later, I needed one as a child, and they provided it. I did not know then which path to take or even what I was looking for. To this day I'm still not sure if we were poor or broke. But I learned to think big and to brew in my own imagination a vision of a better life. I just had to go out and pursue it.

Chapter 2

KNOW WHO YOU ARE

Milton Academy was not just a different place. It was a different planet. I was suddenly around people who had second and third homes and household staffs, who traveled frequently to remote countries, and who poured tea with gloved hands. The language was foreign: *summer* was used as a verb. My family's middle-class aspirations had certainly not prepared me for Milton. It seemed we just skipped that passage. These people were *rich*.

I thought I had been sent to Milton by mistake, as if some clerical error had dispatched me accidentally to an enchanted land, and I lived in dread that someone would discover the lapse. What I didn't appreciate at first was that all the boys were trying to find their own path. In my case, I had to learn to bridge two starkly different worlds. Each had a claim on me and insisted that, to be authentic, I had to choose one over the other. I learned, like everyone, that life is full of choices, but I came to suspect that most of them were false. Authenticity is a matter of values. Know those and be true to them, and you can comfortably navigate the uneven terrain of life.

I arrived in Boston on a sun-kissed September afternoon in 1970, one of those soft, still New England days when the autumn colors are just beginning to appear. A blue van, with an orange M on its side, collected me and a few other kids from Logan Airport and drove us through the city toward our new home. I said nothing as I stared out the window. From the elevated central artery, the Boston on view did not seem like much of a city. The downtown was a few stolid gray buildings of modest height compared to those in Chicago. As we passed the sign that said EN-TERING MILTON, all pretensions of a city were abandoned. On the hill across a salt marsh where small wooden boats floated listlessly stood large homes on large lawns with large spaces between them.

Suddenly our driver shouted, "Here we are!" On the right, he pointed to the boys' school; on the left, the girls' school. As we passed the library, we came upon the main green at the center of the campus. I had never seen so much private lawn in my life. The whole place breathed of tradition and privilege. Surrounding the perfectly manicured grass were stately brick buildings with clean white trim, Doric and Ionic columns, and ivy creepers. The huge elm and maple trees, which seemed to have been there since Creation, added a sense of entrenchment and stability. The structures themselves—Forbes House, Wigglesworth Hall, Straus Library—taught me an early lesson: The graduates never really die; they just turn into buildings.

At the far end of the lawn, on its own grassy knoll, was Hallowell House, my new residence. Though it had a Georgian Colonial exterior like the rest of the campus, it was Milton's newest dormitory, built in the 1960s, and lacked the hoary charm of the older halls, with their dark wood paneling and window seats. It did have "alcoves" in common with the other boys' dorms, the warren of spaces on the top floors where the eighth- and ninth-graders lived. Arriving shortly before dinner, I was starving. The other boys had left for the dining hall already, but I wasn't sure what to do or say, and I didn't want to walk in last. So I stayed in my quarters. It was just as well. I had time to explore.

My room itself was spartan. Instead of walls, fixed dividers that did not reach the ceiling separated uniform spaces. There was a curtain in place of a door. Each alcove had a single twin bed made of steel with a hard mattress; a plain but sturdy wooden bureau, desk, and chair; and a shallow, built-in closet with another curtain across the front. The floor was cold, bare, and institutional. I didn't have enough clothes to fill the bureau. The bathroom with its common shower was down the hall.

I had a single window, just like at home. But instead of an air shaft and the view of our neighbor's window a few feet away, this window opened onto that same lush park in the center of the campus. I could see nearly a half mile of green, gold, and red. I couldn't believe I had my own bed and no longer had to sleep on the floor every third night. Most of the kids complained about their room, as they were used to more lavish accommodations. I thought it was sublime.

On that first day of class the next morning, I just wanted to fit in, but it wasn't easy. The dress code required that boys wear jackets and ties to class. When the clothing list had arrived at home the summer before, my grandparents splurged on a new jacket for me. But a jacket in our world was a Windbreaker, so when the other boys at Milton were donning their blue blazers and tweed coats, I emerged in my dark blue Windbreaker, off the rack from Sears.

Clearly, I had a lot to learn, starting with the actual learning. I was used to being the prized pupil, but now I was intellectually adrift. In my freshman English class, it seemed that the other boys had already read many of the classics and could cross-reference other texts that I had barely even heard of. I was intimidated and embarrassed. I also read more slowly and was constantly

behind. I received my first C, on a short writing assignment, and was demoralized.

I was even more astray in my foreign language class.
When I was told that it was Latin, I smiled and thought,
"You have *got* to be kidding." Our teacher, a kindly man
with thin white hair, translucent skin, and a dry voice that
made you want to take a drink of water, was widely presumed by his students to have been around when Latin
was still spoken. He used Latin phrases when he gave us
direction, such as *magna cum celeritate* for "hurry up."

It appeared that the work in his class had no connection whatsoever to life outside that classroom, save for
the ability to translate the inscriptions on the crests of
other elite schools. Strange indeed. But the cadences were
similar to those in the King James Bible, which was standard reading at home. Studying Shakespeare for the first
time was a similar experience: exotic and inscrutable at
first until I stumbled across swear words that I thought my
grandmother had invented. When I heard her call someone a "son of a mongrel bitch," it seemed like such an original putdown until I read it in Shakespeare. At least Gram
was profane in a learned way.

Beyond the classroom lay a class-conscious minefield.
I tried to befriend other students, but their worldliness,
their aura of entitlement, reinforced my own insecurities.
One boy commuted from home in an antique Rolls-Royce.
Another took ski vacations to Switzerland. Some bore the
same surnames as the buildings. Many had traveled or lived

on multiple continents. They all seemed to know the code of dress, language, and manners.

The very confidence I lacked seemed to come naturally to everyone else. It was at Milton that I first observed how self-assured the rich so often appear about everything and everyone else, as if wealth were a substitute for experience. I cannot count the number of times I sat at the dinner table of a classmate and listened respectfully to a parent's dissertation on the causes of black poverty or family breakdown, only to be asked by that parent if he or she could touch my hair, wondering what it felt like.

Race, of course, was its own complex dynamic. Back home, we would make fun of the way white people spoke, with their distinctive nasal sounds and their use of such words as *guy* and *pal*, terms we would never use. Now I was outnumbered. I was the one who spoke funny, and I was often on the defensive.

Some of the slights were relatively harmless. I was called "nigger" once by an English teacher who thought he was just being familiar. The larger problem was how Milton actually interpreted racial integration: More often than not, it was a one-way street. I was expected to absorb and display the ways and habits of this monochromatic culture, to adapt until I fit in, but I was not expected to contribute to that culture, to enrich it by sharing my own experience. I was welcome in that new world, it seemed, so long as I did not bring too much of my old world along.

It was impossible to explain any of this to my family

back home. In early, infrequent phone calls, after the initial excitement of hearing my mother's voice, I would lapse into an awkward silence. "How are you?" was followed by an obligatory "Fine" and little more. As a parent, I have come to know how natural that is. But at the time it seemed I had a lot to say without the vocabulary to express it.

When I returned to the South Side for my first Christmas break, I began to realize how difficult it would be to balance my two worlds. As I was greeted by my family in our front hall, Rhonda looked me over and deadpanned, "He talks like a white boy." Gram shot her a look and replied, "He speaks like an educated boy."

My mother and grandparents had had no real idea what they were sending me off to, beyond a vague notion that it was a better opportunity in safer surroundings. Their eyes glazed over when I tried to tell them details about my experiences back East. My friends were variously indifferent and resentful. "What's an ambassador?" one of them asked with a sneer, as I tried to describe the foreign service family of an eighth-grader at Milton. I had to confess that I didn't really know. The truth is, I could no more explain Milton to my family and friends on the South Side than I could explain the South Side to my peers at Milton. Understanding the difference required more effort than either side wanted to give.

My father hated the very idea of prep school. Milton was only a few hours' train ride from New York, so I saw more of him when I was there. But during those visits he would make clear his disapproval of my attending Milton. He thought the school would "make me white." He himself was widely read in the Black Power literature of the late 1960s and feared that I would forget that ours was a heritage of struggle and pain for which whites were to blame. He was concerned that I would lose a sense of who I was. In his view, my identity as a young black man was defined by white oppression. America was profoundly and irredeemably racist, he would say, so pain was inevitable. He worried that I would let my guard down at Milton and open myself to hurt.

He had reason to believe I was naive about race. He knew how hard Gram and Poppy tried to shield us from racism and how my mother had urged us to take people as they come. She had been moved by Martin Luther King Jr. and his message of love and reconciliation. So my father could hardly have been faulted for his wariness. He had seen the way popular black musicians could not patronize the clubs where they performed. He knew the indignities of the road trip. He believed every white record producer exploited the talents of black artists. But I was just a kid hoping to experience the best of the great, wide world without limits, and I was determined to figure out the ways of the world on my own terms.

These were the tensions in my life. My father wanted me to reject the school, and all that it represented, that my mother so desperately and indiscriminately wanted me to embrace, and the school where I wanted to excel didn't seem to have a comfortable place for me. I continued on this wobbly ground, straddling these two worlds, trying not to let the one know much about the other. I was conflicted, worried, and confused. Not every kid survived this dissonance. Once again, I was saved by the love of adults.

My freshman English teacher, Albert Oliver Smith, was extraordinary. The other teachers called him "A.O." or "Toby." Students, current and former, simply called him "Mr. Smith." He was right out of central casting: wizened and bent, with a crew cut that seemed last in fashion in the 1940s and was especially out of place amid the wayward manes of the 1970s. He wore a musty, ill-fitting tweed jacket that smelled of the lit cigarette that was often wedged in the corner of his mouth when he was not in class. With his white Oxford button-down shirt, the collar almost always frayed, he wore plaid knit ties or ones with tiny school seals. With his family's roots dating back to the beginnings of the Bay State in the late seventeenth century, he bore the look of old money. He also had the right résumé. He had attended St. Paul's School and Harvard College, served—for reasons I never understood—in the Royal Air Force during the Second World War, and then, in a telling flash of independence, married Aubrey, a spicy and voluptuous Texan who spoke and taught Spanish.

With only fourteen of us in his class, we could not escape Mr. Smith's demands. (Neither could his pet, which lounged under the table, an old black standard poodle that had evidently never been washed.) If he thought you were dithering in response to his question, he would make the sign of two horns with his pointing and pinkie fingers, indicating "bullshit." He only needed to say the word once or twice at the beginning of the semester. After that, the gesture was enough. His other tactic was to make you stand, face the class, and recite, "I am ignorant, Mr. Smith." He believed that no one learned until they acknowledged what they *didn't* know.

I struggled in the class, yet it was magic. Mr. Smith spoke musically, with total command of the language. He remains the most fluent English speaker I have ever heard. He insisted that one's writing and speech be energetic and precise. Find just the right word. Shun pretense and ambiguity. Simple sentences are best, and when you finish writing them, read them aloud—which we did when we read Shakespeare, then other plays or prose. He taught us that written language, at its best, has a rhythm and timbre that is every bit as powerful as the musical riffs that my father played. Perhaps not surprisingly, this old Yankee also loved jazz.

Over a long weekend, when the other boys were off to their family retreats and overseas junkets, Mr. Smith invited me to go with him and his family to Cape Cod. The land on Pleasant Bay in South Orleans had been "in the family" (another new expression for me) for generations, and the Smiths had built a weekend home near the water a few years earlier. When I asked the housemaster for permission to go, he raised his eyebrows in surprise and told me this was an "important invitation." Mr. Smith was revered among the faculty. I should appreciate the honor and significance of being asked.

Of course, this did nothing to help me relax. When Mr. Smith picked me up at the dorm in his battered green Ford station wagon, with his slightly younger children in the backseat, I was a bundle of nerves. Katherine and Peter were just as awkward at first, but we loosened up with games on the drive down. The Smiths had a tradition of competing to be the first to glimpse the Sagamore Bridge when coming around the last bend south on Route 3. The winner got to decide whether to stop for ice cream. Mr. Smith usually won, so the stops were rare.

At the very end of a long, narrow road, which offered glimpses of the bay as we got closer, we arrived at their driveway, which wound down a hill to their simple, lovely home. It was dusk on a cool, cloudless evening, and the glow was warm through the big glass doors leading into the huge central room with a cathedral ceiling and massive brick fireplace. Aubrey had gone down ahead to open up the house and start dinner. The smell of the wood fire and marinated chicken charring on the grill mixed with the sea breeze coming off the bay. There was red Bordeaux, of which A.O. was a connoisseur. He showed me how to hold the glass, judge the "legs" as a measure of the tannin, open the wine up with air, smell for different fruits and elements, and taste it on different parts of the tongue. Who knew? I was all of fourteen, and my sole experience with wine had been Mogen David at Christmas dinner. We were studying the *Odyssey* in class, so when I mentioned a "libation" to honor the occasion, A.O. beamed with a teacher's delight. Their welcome was so warm and natural, and their interest in both finding out who I was and telling me who they were was so genuine, that I still think of them and that weekend as a model of hospitality. A.O. and Aubrey were urbane and conversational with me in a way that no adult had ever really been before. I was supposed to respond and engage, not just say "Yes, ma'am" and "No, sir." But all I really wanted to do was listen.

That first weekend, we were all turning in on Friday night, and A.O. was saying good night to his own children while Aubrey was making sure my bed was comfortable and the towels were fresh. He said "Good night" to Katherine and Peter, adding whatever pet name he conjured for the moment, then told them, "I love you." He then said the very same words to me. He was matter-of-fact, natural, authentic, neither more nor less than he had been with his own children seconds before. It was the first time any man had ever told me he loved me. I had never heard this from Poppy or my own father. For that matter, I had rarely heard it from Gram or my mother. They felt it and expressed it in various ways, to be sure, but saying so out loud and offhandedly was a new experience. I let it wash over me. I did not know what to say in response, but I think my desire to emulate A.O.—his emotional candor, his generosity of spirit—started then and there.

A. O. Smith deeply influenced many students over the years, forming bonds and lighting intellectual fires. In my case, I think he recognized that I needed someone to help me navigate my new world and that I was eager to learn everything about it. That I respected authority and tradition in an era of rebellion and defiance surely strengthened our friendship (which lasted until the end of his life, fifteen years later). My difficulties at Milton didn't end after that weekend, but I no longer felt like an outsider.

If A. O. Smith became my surrogate father, then June Elam was my surrogate mother. In the early 1970s, June was an upper-middle-class black resident of Milton, a rarity. All three of her children were students at the school. I now joke that I started out dating her elder daughter and ended up in love with her mother, but that's not much of an exaggeration. Tall, with sharp features and a small, intimate voice, June is the most giving individual I have ever known. The first time I met her, late in my sophomore year, in 1972, she asked for my mother's telephone number. She promptly called and told my mother to take comfort in knowing that another black family lived only a mile from Deval's dormitory and he would always be welcome in their home. My mother said that call was the answer to her prayers.

June was that for me, as well, in ways large and small. I had trouble finding a barber nearby, so she drove me to Roxbury, a largely black neighborhood in Boston. I delivered newspapers on and near the campus, and during one brutal snowstorm she drove me to all my customers. I did what I could to reciprocate. Using oversized poster boards, I created a Mother's Day card for her with a sentimental inscription. Once I saved enough money to hire a limousine to take us to a famous seafood restaurant in Cohasset. She made a point of amicably protesting these actions, but I took great pride in showing my gratitude.

June seemed undeterred by the same racial contradictions that initially bedeviled me at Milton. She was married to a politically connected lawyer from a prominent Roxbury family and lived in a sprawling ranch house on a landscaped acre. In Milton, she attended parents' meetings, teas, and dinner parties; in Roxbury, she participated in church and community gatherings. Her personality seemed to transcend place. She was exactly the same giving, open soul wherever she happened to be.

She seemed to treat race as other people's problem. If I walked through town to her home, I would almost invariably be stopped by the police and asked for identification. It was humiliating to have to explain that I was just walking to a friend's house or to the convenience store and was not the thief they presumed I was, casing the neighborhood. It helped a little when the school issued identification cards. Once a cruiser pulled up behind another student and me when we were strolling on Randolph Avenue and put on his blue lights. A young, gruff officer with sunglasses swaggered over to us, asking what business we had in the neighborhood. "We're just walking up to the Curtiss Compact," I said. When he asked for identification, I took unnatural pride in displaying my card, showing I was in fact a resident. After many months of this ritual, however, my pride turned into resentment at having to show identification at all. June seemed to take it all in stride. "That's their problem," she'd say. "You know who you are, don't you?"

At that moment, I'm not certain I did know exactly who I was or where I belonged, but I was feeling more comfortable with myself and the different worlds I was straddling.

June herself was working her way through an unhappy divorce. She was worried about the impact on her own kids, so we spent hours talking about what my parents' separation was like for Rhonda and me. It helped her, but it also helped me recall and retire many feelings. Like Λ. O. and Aubrey Smith, June was conspicuous with her love. What I had been missing! I drank it in.

In my senior year, I was sitting in trigonometry class one morning when one of my classmates walked in with a hangdog look and sat down next to me as the teacher began his calculations at the board. Will Speers was a year behind me, and I didn't know him well, but I saw he was hurting. Motioning with my hands, I asked what was wrong. Will picked up a tall Styrofoam cup left over from midmorning coffee and wrote on it: "She doesn't like me anymore." I then took the cup and wrote something back. He responded with another message. The cup went back and forth, and by the time the class was over, the woes of Will's entire love life had been etched across that Styrofoam.

Thus began a friendship that became a defining experience for me at Milton. We became, and are to this day, close friends, even though we're from polar opposite worlds. Will could trace his roots to the earliest English settlers; grew up in affluent New Canaan, Connecticut; and would soon be the third generation of his family to attend Princeton. Despite our very different backgrounds, we both had open minds. We shared an interest in books (American and British). We were both enchanted and intimidated by pretty girls. We just connected.

That winter, we decided to take a Greyhound bus to his family's one-room cabin on Squam Lake in New Hampshire. Will told his parents about our plan and got their permission. *Deval* is a gender-neutral name, so several days before we were to leave, Will's parents called him and asked, "You *are* going with a guy, aren't you?"

Left unsaid was that I was black. His parents are strong liberals, so Will did not expect a problem. It just never occurred to him to mention my race. But he was hypersensitive nonetheless. When the bus dropped us off in front of the bowling alley in the tiny, snow-covered hamlet of

Holderness, at the foothills of the White Mountains, "Uncle Erk" White, an old friend of Will's family, was there to pick us up. "Hello, boy," he greeted me warmly as I stepped off the bus. Will was mortified.

"He calls everybody 'boy,'" Will told me nervously. "Don't worry."

I smiled and told him to relax. I was learning to shrug off slights, real or perceived, and in this case none was taken. I was just glad Uncle Erk could meet us on that frigid winter evening and take us to the cabin.

I was not quite eighteen, not old enough to buy alcohol legally, but I prevailed on an older student to purchase a six-pack of beer and a few bottles of wine for our trip. They were snug in our backpacks with our other supplies as we piled into Uncle Erk's truck. With Will in the front seat next to Uncle Erk and me in the back, we bounced along rutted roads for miles, and the bottles in my backpack started to clink guiltily against each other.

"You gotta lotta glass back there," Uncle Erk observed.

Will, in a panic, searched for an explanation. "Yeah," he said. "We're bringing a lot of mayonnaise on our trip."

I did all I could to stifle my laughter.

My good humor ended when we reached the end of our ride. Uncle Erk let us out at the end of an unplowed road that led a mile or more down to the lakeside fishing cabin where we would stay. We faced at least two feet of snow. We strapped on snowshoes, hoisted our packs, and started to hike down by moonlight. It was unspeakably

cold and a little unnerving. What was a city kid from the
South Side doing in the deep woods at night on snowshoes
with a heavy backpack? But I got into the rhythm of the
walk, and soon enough we arrived at the cabin, found the
key, and settled in. We lit a roaring fire, which would blaze
for most of our stay; in my sleeping bag I would snuggle up
as close to it as possible on those frigid nights. The next
morning, we used a pickax to cut a hole in the frozen lake
for water to drink and cook with.

Squam Lake and its people meant a lot to Will, and
still do. He had known the place all his life and felt a
special bond that he wanted to share. During the day, we
hiked around the woods and explored some of his favorite
spots. We slogged up to Uncle Erk's house and drank cocoa
with him and his wife. The landscape was glorious. The
experience of the snowshoes, cross-country skiing across
the frozen cove, cooking steaks over a fireplace, reading
silently by candlelight, not washing for days, being cold at
night—it was all so new. I could not even pretend to be a
woodsman. Will was clearly in charge.

We spent much of our time talking about girls and our
failed or hoped-for romances, though we also talked about
books, family, friends, and whatever dreams we had for the
future. His father and grandfather were both Presbyterian
ministers, and there was a spirituality about Squam Lake
that he had come to revere. Mostly I listened. I received
a lot more than I gave that weekend. I was still not quite
ready to describe my life before Milton, and I wasn't sure

Will was ready to hear about it. We were two boys trying to figure out how to become men, and we had just enough "mayonnaise" to get us through.

Ultimately, the more time I spent at Milton—at tea parties after football games, at alumni council gatherings—the more comfortable I became. I was never popular or much of an athlete. I was just a good citizen, a patient listener, and a sharp observer. I figured out the blue blazer and the rep tie, the difference between the old money destinations and the new. Though I had never actually been to most of these places or even owned a rep tie, I had broken the code. I could out-WASP the WASPs. I could even use *summer* as a verb.

As I learned the code, people grew more comfortable with me. They opened up and allowed me to see how universal the human condition really is. Despite their venerable names and magnificent homes and important art collections, the men and women of privilege bore struggles hardly different from those I had seen at home. They told me about their bad marriages, their estranged children, their family traumas. There was alcoholism, addiction, infidelity, suicide, ruin, and loss. One student got pregnant during her senior year and decided to keep the baby. The father of another could not keep a job and spent most of his days in his pajamas, staring out his bedroom window at the garden. Money may have helped some of these people cope with calamity, but it did not immunize anyone from it.

Though I was largely accepted at Milton, true assimilation was not possible. It was as if I was encouraged to forget my past and embrace a community that would not actually let me surrender that past. Sometimes, as my father feared, I let my guard down.

In my junior year, I was the student manager of the soda machines in the dorms and the candy concession at the Canteen, which was open at morning break for students. The money went to the scholarship fund, with a small cut to the student manager (who was always a scholarship student). I collected the money and paid for the sales stock in arrears. But in one instance, the funds did not cover the soda bill. When I told the deliveryman that I was short, he took the matter to the dean of students, who took it to the housemaster and ultimately the headmaster. We had a round of questioning, and the authorities insinuated that I had stolen the money. I had not taken a dime, of course, nor had I even been paid what I was owed, as a thorough review of the books made clear. I explained, however, that I had heard the boys boast of being able to reach into the vending machines to pull a can out and had actually seen a few do it. The masters dropped the issue when one of the boys blithely demonstrated that it could be done quite easily, and no evidence could be found that

I had enriched myself. But there were no apologies. "Boys will be boys" was the reaction to the white kids stealing sodas from the machine. "Watch yourself" was the message to me.

It was the first time I'd felt the helplessness and hurt of false accusation. I knew that such an accusation could jeopardize my standing at Milton. The presumption that the actual thieves—the rich white boys who were helping themselves to sodas—were innocent pranksters while I—the black kid on scholarship—was up to no good stung me deeply. When I tried to explain why I was so upset to a young and caring white teacher, he explained a rationale that had nothing to do with race—in effect, why I was the logical suspect. I had control of the money, so it was natural to question me closely, even if I was otherwise beyond reproach. He was trying to comfort me, to keep me from being bitter. But I then appreciated that the curse of being black is always having to wonder whether the things that go wrong in your life are on account of your race.

That was part of the burden, the insecurity, of straddling these two worlds, and I could only do it by being true to myself. I was part of both communities, and they were part of me. I certainly did not give up on the people at Milton whom I had come to love. I became a loyal graduate, a trustee, a benefactor, eventually a parent of two students, and a mentor to many other scholarship students. But somehow I knew back then, even during the stirring lectures and quiet revelations, that I would get a great education at the risk of a broken heart.

By the time I went on to Harvard, it was easier to find my bearings in a place that I once would not have been able to contemplate. I knew the basic geography, of course; Harvard Square was at the opposite end of the Red Line from Milton and a frequent destination on weekend excursions with other students. And I was a Milton man at Harvard, after all, surprisingly but indisputably part of a long tradition, so I thought I had a leg up. My freshman roommates were eager young men from Alabama, Iowa, New Jersey, and Belmont, a wealthy suburb of Boston. All of us were afraid of failing or being outed as admissions mistakes, so we worked hard. On the weekends, we dated Wellesley women and went to movies and drank too much. I was trying to belong, to forge an identity, but even at Harvard I could not escape the temptation of false choices.

As a sophomore I was "punched," or recruited, for one of the Finals Clubs, all-male relics from the days when the campus had no dining facilities. These private social clubs were filled mainly by the wealthy legacy students who had attended private schools. Apparently, one once joined the Hasty Pudding Club as a freshman and took one's meals there. Then you moved on to your "final" club, where you dined with other members, presumably of the same social set. After a tortured period of being courted at fancy lunches and dinners and rejecting invitations, I finally joined the Fly Club. Roosevelts and Kennedys had passed through the wide door into those cool, dark rooms, so why not me? Even so, except for an occasional black-tie dinner or garden party with the graduates, a cast of marvelous New England characters, I hardly ever went near the place. It was just too expensive and too weird: servants older than my father dressed in livery waiting on nineteen-year-olds, refreshing our drinks and serving us lunch. I should have known something was wrong when I felt embarrassed and apologetic about going into the building. At the time, I just wanted to be validated by one world or the other. In fact, I seemed eligible for neither.

Still, my experience at Harvard was far more positive than not. I made some close friends, and through them, through professors who opened more new worlds for us, and through mentors who inspired us, we burrowed ahead in our effort to be considered part of the elite, which pleased my mother as much as it appalled my father.

I graduated on an overcast day, but I was elated. I was about to join a storied group. My grandparents, mother, and sister came, as did Mrs. Quaintance, my sixth-grade teacher. Their pride and enthusiasm reminded me why this journey mattered.

Later that evening, after graduation was over, we all went out to dinner at a restaurant on Boston Harbor. It was a fun but low-key evening: Everyone was pretty worn out from the abundant festivities Harvard offered to

soften us up to become grateful and generous lifelong do-
nors. I caught Rhonda looking at me strangely throughout
dinner, and I suspected she was again judging how far I
was from what I was supposed to become. She had finished high school, lived in her own apartment, and was
working on her cosmetology license. She was living on
the South Side and making her way. I was graduating from
a prestigious college with no certain plan except to travel
overseas. We were clearly on different paths.

After dinner, Rhonda pulled me aside, looked me
in the eye, and said softly, "I am so proud of you." Then
she burst into tears. We held each other, crying, for many
minutes, heaving our sobs of joy and forgiveness, letting
go of the years of judgment and jealousy, accepting each
other for who and what we were. Much more would be said
in endless conversations that summer and in subsequent
years, but nothing else was really needed.

Some people will always believe that, but for Milton, I
would be peddling drugs or gangbanging on the South Side
of Chicago. I reject that. Even back home, others had high
expectations for me, and I had them for myself. Milton was a
launching pad, but I always had some spring in my legs. Like
Milton, Harvard exposed me both to great privilege and to
the folly of equating that with fulfillment or salvation.

For some time, I thought the lesson of my years at Milton or even Harvard was that you had to adapt to your new

environment, learn the code, if you were going to belong. But eventually I came to see that belonging has nothing to do with place. It has to do with purpose, with values. The expectations of the South Side and Milton Academy implied a choice: Be of one or the other, but not both, because they inherently conflict. That choice, however, was false and was totally unsuited for the world I wanted to experience and be part of.

I learned to focus less on where I was and more on who I am. Candor, compassion, generosity of spirit, curiosity, and learning to listen, as Louis Pasteur once wrote, "without losing your temper or your self-confidence"—these were the qualities I wanted and that I would always try to carry with me. These became the points on my compass.

That decision carries risk. It is easier to follow someone else's star, some well-worn and recognized path. Strangers and loved ones alike question nonconformists and often true independence itself. But I have come to love taking risks, even those that seem to defy all logic. Once you take personal responsibility for your choices, once you let your values lead you, the journey itself—be it through an unfamiliar school or on a campaign trail—can be wondrous. Eventually you'll connect with those who share your vision. You'll find or form a community of those with similar values. And that is reward enough. Leaping into the unknown can be enriching beyond measure if, as Poppy would say, you "remember who you are and what you represent."

Chapter 3

Dean Jeremy Knowles used to tell a story about a sculpture in Harvard Yard, by the renowned British artist Henry Moore, which sits on the green next to Lamont Library. "Standing in front of it on the path or gazing at it from the library, it looks pretty lumpy," he would say to incoming freshmen. "A bunch of massive golden shapes, quite attractive, but meaningless, and mostly good for photographing small children in. But go out of the gate onto Quincy Street and turn left, and look back through the thirty-fourth gap in the second set of railings. Suddenly you will see a splendid and voluptuous work."

He'd ask the students, "What's the moral?" His answer: If you don't understand something, the reason may be that you are simply standing in the wrong place. "So if you don't understand a theorem in physics or a passage from *Ulysses* or a Schoenberg trio or your roommate's politics, remember Henry Moore," he'd say, "and try a new perspective."

My move from the South Side to Milton had given me some insight into Dean Knowles's point. Though less jarring, so had the transition from Milton to Harvard. I had learned how culture explains why people sometimes draw different conclusions from the same information, and I continued to be fascinated by the complexities of what unites us and what divides us. I've always tried to be a student of humanity, which required a much broader horizon, an unpredictable canvas, an exposure to disparate environments, ideas, and perspectives. I decided I needed more practice at understanding and transcending differences, and I needed it before launching a career.

I was also not quite sure exactly what career I wanted. That was not unusual for college graduates in 1978, but less so for Harvard graduates. My classmates were driven and focused, with careers and, in many cases, pathways through life that already seemed set in stone. They were on their way to medical school or graduate school or jobs in finance, industry, or the arts. I was more flexible. Business school seemed like a good option because I liked management, but I was really not strong enough in math to be a compelling candidate. Nor was I ready to commit to law school, which one friend described as "the great sloth bin of the undecided." I considered a calling in the clergy and even filled out an application for Union Seminary in New York. But I wasn't certain about that path either.

Another possibility arose when a career counselor told me about the Michael Clark Rockefeller Traveling Fellowship. Michael was the son of Nelson Rockefeller, the former vice president and governor of New York. After graduating from Harvard, Michael went on to explore the anthropology of New Guinea and brought home extraordinary artifacts and information about the Papuan people. He also wrote beautifully about how the experience had affected him personally. Tragically, and under unclear circumstances, he perished on a return trip to New Guinea. In his memory, his family established the fellowship to enable an individual to spend a year in a distinctly non-Western culture. It embodied the virtues of discovery and perspective that had become important to me, so I applied. The stipend itself was just enough money to get there and back—presumably so no one could move into an Intercontinental Hotel. For fellows, the bracing realities of Third World countries would not include room service. The point was to make your way in unfamiliar settings.

Applicants had to stipulate where they wanted to travel and why. Having never been overseas, I had no frame of reference. I chose Sudan because I had written about it when interning at banks in New York and Boston during the summers in college. More than twenty years later, Sudan, and Darfur in particular, would be known for its bloody civil war, which led to one of the worst humanitarian disasters in memory. But when I was applying for the fellowship, all I knew was that Sudan was the largest country in Africa as well as the poorest. It was in many ways still "uncharted" and a focus of increasing attention from international development lenders. I was curious about the impact of economic development on cultural and social norms and who takes responsibility for the disruption of those norms. It was enough to earn me an interview.

I met with the selection committee in a small basement conference room at the career center. The chair, a tall, distinguished anthropology professor with bushy gray brows and deep crow's-feet that framed his eyes, seemed skeptical but amused. He quizzed me about my personal story and observed that I had already adjusted to an unfamiliar culture by coming to Milton Academy from the South Side of Chicago. True enough, I said, but I wanted to stretch my boundaries even further and was committed to exploring a truly foreign land. At the end of the interview, paraphrasing Pasteur, he said, "Chance favors the well prepared." Well prepared or not, I got my chance.

As a Rockefeller fellow, I was responsible for creating much of my own program, and that meant finding an employer.

I wrote to everyone I knew with a contact in Africa, specifically in Sudan. Relief agencies, banks, universities, volunteer organizations—you name it. I sent scores of letters and received one reply. A man who worked for a United Nations Development Programme project in Khartoum wrote a friendly letter saying that he was not sure what I would do when I got there, but he would figure it out and I should come. I set about applying for my first passport, arranging for the necessary visas, getting the inoculations, buying a backpack, and figuring out how to fit a year's worth of clothing and personal effects into it.

Meanwhile, Will Speers had just finished his junior year at Princeton and was making summer plans. Now that I would be taking my first trip overseas, we decided to spend the summer together, trekking around England and Scotland, before I ventured on to Africa. Will had visited England with his family a few years before and had a passing familiarity with parts of it. Its culture was different from America's, but not radically so. At least everyone spoke a language that sounded familiar, so starting there would make a smoother transition for my year abroad.

Before we left, the admissions director at Milton told us that a young student from Edinburgh would be coming to spend a year at the school, sight unseen, and asked us to stop by his family's home and answer any questions they might have. When we arrived in Edinburgh, we contacted Ian and Esme Walker, whose son, Angus, would be the lucky new Miltonian. Though Angus was away, his parents promptly invited us to lunch at their grand, eighteenth-century manor house in the "old" section of town, and that led to a lifelong friendship. We had six weeks like that: befriending strangers, seeing the sights, figuring out how to drive on the wrong side of the road, and managing the currency.

But at summer's end, Will flew home, and Sudan was staring me in the face. As I saw him off from Heathrow, I suddenly realized that I was on my own, and I was momentarily overwhelmed.

"One foot in front of the other," I whispered to myself. "One foot in front of the other."

Khartoum, the capital of Sudan, sits at the confluence of the Blue and White Niles, and it was hard to get to in those days. The flight from London made numerous stops and was expensive. A gradual introduction to life on the African continent seemed to make more sense. My correspondent at the UNDP was expecting me anytime in September, so why not take the long way, via Cairo? The cheapest route to Cairo went through Athens. So I flew there and spent several days walking around that extraordinary city, seeing the sights and waiting for the weekly flight to Egypt's capital. It was the first time I had been alone in a place where nothing was familiar—not the language, the signs, the food, or the surroundings. I was scared and excited at the same time. I don't think I slept at all.

The flight from Athens was delayed, so we landed in Cairo late at night. The airport was apparently closed.

Ill-tempered immigration officials flanked by gruff soldiers with black metal machine guns checked passports and visas. On the other side of the checkpoint was pure chaos. Crowds of waiting men were screaming at the baggage handlers. The baggage handlers were screaming at the passengers. The passengers were screaming at the taxi drivers. The guards were screaming at the crowds and trying to hold them back. It was madness in at least two languages. What had I gotten myself into?

I had memorized a handful of Arabic greetings and numbers from a phrase book during the flight. When I stepped up to present my passport, I screwed up my courage and said, "*Salaam alaikum,*" the most traditional Arabic greeting. The sullen official, sitting there in his black beret and dull green uniform, complete with epaulets, looked again at my American passport and back at me with surprise and smiled broadly, revealing brown-stained teeth under his black mustache. He replied heartily, "*Alaikum salaam.*" Chattering away in Arabic, he left his post, despite the long line of passengers behind me, to help me claim my backpack and push through the crowd to the curb. He then hailed one of the decrepit taxis and spoke to the driver. He seemed to be admonishing the driver not to take advantage of me. I felt reassured. I didn't know where I was going and had no idea what the man actually said, but gestures of kindness need no translation.

I didn't have a plan. I couldn't afford to check into a big Western-style hotel, and it wasn't in the spirit of the fellowship anyway. So, using my phrase book and a guide-book called *Africa on the Cheap,* or something like that, I asked the driver to take me to a cheap hotel downtown. At least I think that's what I asked him. We lurched from the curb and headed to the center of the city, the springs in the shabby seat poking me in the butt, and the thin sheet metal loosely covering the old Renault's repairs flapping with every bounce.

After a short spin on a highway, the taxi crept slowly through narrow streets with throngs of people and live-stock everywhere. To say it's hot in Cairo in the summer is an understatement, so the residents come out in the cooler evenings and stay well into the night. The cafés overflowed. The shops were open, and patrons were hag-gling over goods. I could smell the sweat through the open taxi windows. Every once in a while, a biker carrying sheep hides, the heads still attached, knocked into the side of the cab. Each time I jumped.

Eventually we pulled up in front of the Ambassador Hotel, a grimy, stucco, seven- or eight-story building. I paid the fare, swung my backpack over my shoulder, and walked in. Men in white *gallabiyas,* traditional full-length cotton shirts, and white head wraps lounged in the unadorned and uncarpeted lobby, sipping tea and chatting. Two fans tried vainly to stir the thick air through the crowded quarters. In my jeans, T-shirt, backpack, and brown skin, I looked at once familiar and unfamiliar. The conversation stopped conspicuously when I walked in. I was just too tired and too on edge to engage. In phrase-book Arabic, I asked for a room, was given an ancient skeleton key from the front desk, and stepped into an obviously unsafe elevator with an attendant. I could hear the conversation in the lobby resume loudly as soon as the door closed. I checked into a filthy room with a single stained mattress on a metal frame, a concrete floor, a window that opened onto the elevator shaft, and a cold-water tap. The bathroom, down the hall, consisted of a hole in the floor over which one stood or squatted and from which the foulest stench rose without relief. None of it mattered. I was asleep in minutes.

I explored the city for a few days. The year 1978 was a good time to be an American in the Middle East. While I was in Cairo, Anwar Sadat, the Egyptian president, came home from signing the popular Camp David Accords in Washington, D.C., and the United States was seen as an honest broker in the long struggle to bring peace to the region. When the Egyptians I met figured out I was American, they were especially gracious.

I got around mainly on foot, wandering for hours through little lanes and city squares. From the main square in the center of Cairo, I squeezed onto a dilapidated public bus. *Crowded* doesn't begin to describe it. People sat on top of each other inside or hung from the windows or doors outside. The bus never really stopped so much as slowed down so that passengers could jump on or off. You paid the fare by passing money from hand to hand to the conductor, the way Americans pay for hot dogs and beer at baseball games. I rode out to Giza and, rounding the last bend in the road, watched the pyramids and the Sphinx rise out of the desert and thrust themselves into the bluest sky. I visited the Cairo Museum, which had more priceless treasure than there was space to properly display and preserve it. I learned to negotiate for everything.

Temperatures were well over 100 degrees during the day, and my clothes seemed to be melting. So did my skin. I still bear scars from the blisters that appeared on my arms just below my T-shirt sleeves. I had been warned about drinking the water, so I had iodine pills to kill the bacteria in my water bottle. They also made the water taste foul, which deterred me from drinking as much as I should have. I was so lightheaded and parched after one day of wandering around the city that I literally stumbled into the lobby of a hotel and collapsed into a booth in the dark, cool bar, disoriented and barely able to speak. I hated beer, but I asked for one anyway. They brought a tall brown bottle without a label that the waiter called *Bira Jamil*, camel's beer. It was icy cold. And divine.

Because I couldn't speak the language and knew no one, conversation was rare, giving me plenty of time to think. My father was on my mind a lot in Cairo. In a manifestation of his militancy, he associated himself with ancient Egyptian culture and took pride that advances in science, engineering, architecture, and art originated among Africans who looked like him. I shared that pride. I also learned to see that what looked like chaos (such as the ride on that bus or the customs in the market) had an internal order once you broke the code.

I felt a new pride in America, too. I had always known the lump-in-the-throat patriotism when the national anthem was played at official occasions or when we said the Pledge of Allegiance at Cub Scout meetings. And certainly the tangible appreciation that people on the street expressed for America's role in the Camp David Accords helped me see that our real power is moral authority. I was proud of that. Still am. But also in Cairo, for the first time in my life, I experienced what it was like to be seen as simply an American, not a category of American. Just as every traveler learns to think anew about home, it was the first time I was ever able to look back at my own home without the filter of race, to reflect on my country as a fully invested citizen, because that was how I was treated by Egyptians.

After several days, I took a train south, traveling along the Nile to Luxor, to see the Valley of the Kings, where some five hundred years ago tombs were built for royalty and nobles. I then headed farther south to Aswan, where I booked space on the open deck of a ferry to float south on Lake Nasser to the Sudanese border. The ferry consisted of several flatbed barges lashed together, groaning and listing under the weight of too many people and too much of their livestock and cargo. Even a small wave could have swamped us—which in fact has happened on occasion.

I was a curiosity, but not a scary one. Travelers, I was

learning, bond quickly. We shared food, water, and tea, as well as conversation, and the calm of the other passengers surprised me. Still, the boat's safety was clearly precarious. If we sank and drowned, no one would have known. My last message home was a newsy letter sent from the Aswan post office just before we boarded. But the other passengers did not seem afraid, so taking my cue from them, neither was I. The evening indeed brought peace, a relief from the day's glaring sun and searing heat. The engine purred smoothly and the vessel rocked gently under shimmering stars. I slept soundly on deck.

The voyage took three days. We finally beached; and the crew, pointing south across the dunes toward absolutely nothing, announced we had arrived in Sudan. I strapped on my backpack and followed the others about a mile or two over the dunes to a small nineteenth-century building surrounded by desert, where a single train track marched bravely into the infinite sand and nameless heat. A narrow-gauge train sat idle and waiting. After a day or two of loading the train with everyone and everything from the barges, we set off south, through the Nubian Desert to Khartoum. The sand on the tracks, combined with the weight of the bodies and cargo, forced the train to a crawl. Dust billowed through the windows on gusts of hot air, mixing with the nutty brine of human odors and the shit smell of live chickens and guinea hens. We stopped five times each day so that the men could alight and pray.

We arrived in Khartoum many days later. Having gone more than a week without a bath, I looked like a piece of the dusty desert we had just crossed. Khartoum was a sprawling version of the tiny towns we had passed through—red mud-brick buildings with corrugated tin roofs, just more of them, punctuated by larger colonial edifices with red tile roofs that signaled officialdom. The occasional electric wire hung from a building's edge, delivering power occasionally. Small white pickup trucks and market lorries (cargo trucks) shared the streets with donkeys, camels, bikes, and men in their *gallabiyas* and skullcaps. The chaotic din, especially in the marketplace (*souk*), and the pungent breeze of animals, musk, and cumin flooded the senses.

I thought of the trips I had made back in the States, on planes, trains, or buses, where I would sit alone and rarely connect with anyone around me. That was no longer an option, and I was forced to communicate with people I would have tried to ignore under other circumstances. Desperation, it turns out, is a great icebreaker. A man on the train, for example, had taught me a few Arabic phrases in exchange for my teaching him a few in English. He introduced me to other men, who showed me how to order food at the trackside stands and how to drink hot tea loaded with sugar and mint instead of my nasty, iodinated water. By the time we reached Khartoum, we were an inarticulate posse, talking animatedly around and above one another, comprehending only a fraction of what was said. But connections had been made, and their friendship, however improvised, was a blessing.

With their help, I found the office of the man with whom I had been corresponding about working in Khartoum. The office was in a one-story building off a main street, opposite the sprawling United Nations compound. On a front porch, wooden stools strung with hemp sat around a low wooden table, a place to share tea with colleagues and visitors. The back garden, just visible from the path to the front door, held a latrine and a faucet, which dripped rust-colored water. Sudanese women swept the dirt along the path outside and worked as clerical staff in the office, too, alongside the expatriate Europeans and the development and diplomatic staff. The Westerners wore khaki bush clothes with lots of pockets and dusty boots. The Sudanese women wore colorful fabrics tied around their bodies and draped modestly over their heads. They were warm but indirect, rarely looking you right in the eye.

I was greeted by bad news. The man I had been writing to had left the week before to spend two years in Long Beach, California, and had said nothing to his colleagues about my coming or his plans for me. I sat there, stunned, while the ex-pat staff apologized briskly for the confusion and returned to their work. The Sudanese staff, however, were embarrassed because I was a guest. They beckoned me to sit at the little table on the front porch, served me tea, and inquired with real interest about my travels. They told me where I could rest and wash up. One young man met me after evening prayers and walked me to the *souk* for a simple meal of beans, cheese, and bread.

After several days of trying to recover from the trip and considering what to do next, the Sudanese staff helped me talk my way onto a project. It turned out that there was a youth training initiative intended to provide construction skills to secondary school dropouts in the Darfur region west of Khartoum, near the Chadi frontier. The project was failing, and senior U.N. officials wanted to know why. I was assigned to travel with Kamal Tayfour, another new employee who had just graduated from the University of Khartoum and whose command of English was only a little better than mine of Arabic. Kamal had been hired as part of the U.N. commitment to bring indigenous talent onto the professional staff. Our job was to do field research in the little villages of El Fasher and Nyala. I believed it was essential work. The more likely truth was that the ex-pat staff was just trying to get both of us out of the way.

Kamal and I didn't take to each other initially. The language barrier was only part of the problem. We were about the same age, but he was the son of a senior govern-ment official, while I appeared to have few credentials. He wore Western clothes on his thin frame, plastic san-dals, and a big fake Rolex. His skin was dark brown and smooth, with no signs of hardship, and he had bright brown eyes and the whitest smile. Kamal was quite formal and polite with me, as with other Westerners and educated Sudanese, but he could be condescending and abrupt with the workers and beggars. When we were together, he did not pray according to strict ritual, but he otherwise deferred to the customs of Islam in a secular setting. He never drank or smoked or spoke immodestly to a woman.

Our first destination was El Fasher, but getting there—a distance about the same as that from Boston to Cleveland—was not simple. The town had a small airstrip built during the Second World War, but it was not fenced, and aircraft had no place to refuel. Sudan Airways flew old prop planes with enough range to get from Khartoum to El Fasher and back, but only if the pilot made one approach for taking off and landing and had no trouble en route. Any mistakes would leave the aircraft running on vapors. Meanwhile, goat and camel herders regularly crossed the strip to water their animals. One small plane, while landing, had recently crashed into a camel, which temporarily closed the airstrip. There was no train either. So most people traveled on the lorries that rumbled through the countryside loaded with supplies. Kamal and I asked around the Omdurman *souk* for a lorry that was going to El Fasher. This too required understanding of method and custom. The *souk* was immense, a maze of narrow, mile-long, intersecting lanes lined with shops. No space was wasted. Goods were crammed into every crevice, with produce and spices stacked in neat pyramids. Every category had its own precinct: one area for the vegetable sellers, another for the rug dealers, another for men selling olives in large, briny barrels. One shop or stand would be squeezed right next to another selling the same items, not more than six feet away. Through these passages snaked thousands of people, each yelling at and across one another, engaging or ignoring the insistent offers of rice or typewriters or brightly colored fabric from Belgium.

No one paid the asking price. Haggling was expected, shopping its own art form. You look, you admire, you handle. You ask with amusement, "How much?" and then scoff at the reply, whatever it is. The merchant crisply recites the merits of his product, why his rug weaving is tighter or softer, why her tomatoes are sweeter. You make a counteroffer and wait for a reaction. If the merchant turns away, which is rare, there is nothing more to discuss. If he reacts with almost anything more, you are duty bound to try to agree on a price. Insults are traded. You say the product is garbage. The merchant says the offer is demeaning. If the item is significant (almost anything more than basic food) and the exchanges become heated (which they often do), someone, usually a little boy in rags, is sent for hot tea with sugar and mint so that you can visit awhile, exchange pleasantries, and cool off. Eventually the conversation returns to the item for sale, and there is more haggling. By the time you agree on a price, everyone is laughing. The merchant almost invariably throws in something else as *baksheesh*, a little gift for being a good sport.

The Omdurman *souk*, like every other market I have visited in Africa, had its own transportation hub as well. It was in the center, at the end of what paved road there was. Scores of lorries loaded and unloaded there, refueled or got repairs, the parts often taken and adapted from other vehicles or machines. The drivers were generally the "big men"—literally—of the *souk*, strong and athletic, as they moved cargo and climbed quickly over and across their lorries. They were also men of significance, perhaps because owning one of these trucks was itself a sign of status, and they employed a younger man or two to help with the loading and unloading and the general management of the business.

Each lorry sold passage on top of its cargo. The trick was finding the right destination and the preferred cargo. In our case, we relied on word of mouth to find a lorry going where we needed to go and in good repair with a reputable driver. Once found, we made our own quick inspection of the vehicle, though neither of us really knew what to look for. Finding the right cargo was another matter. Sacks of dried dates, for example, were better than cartons of pots and pans because the dates would provide some cushion for the passengers. After a day or two of interviewing drivers, Kamal settled on a lorry with a mixed cargo of clothing, cookware, and dried spices going our way, and we bargained for space on top. The price settled, we were told to come back before dawn the next day, once all the cargo was loaded, for what would be a four- to five-day ride. We spent the balance of the day gathering enough dates, nuts, bread, and water for the trip and returned the next morning to find the truck piled high and teetering with its cargo lashed under a loose tarp. We set off at daybreak with at least a dozen others high above the cargo.

From the edge of the city, the road west consisted of tracks through the sand. It was well over 100 degrees at midday. Nothing moved on the landscape except us. We were young and old, wearing both Western and indigenous garb, united by our common discomfort. Everyone wore a towel or a broad hat to shield ourselves from the intense sun. We spoke little, as if we were trying to conserve our strength. Communication consisted mostly of smiles of understanding when we hit an especially hard bump. The strain of the engine, downshifting and upshifting, was the only sound for hours.

Early that first evening, several miles outside Khartoum, a freak rainstorm hit. Everything turned to mud, and the truck sank to its axles. We sat there, huddled against the rain, until morning. We were soaked, but no one complained. There were just the same occasional understanding and reassuring smiles. By daybreak, the hard rain stopped, the sun burst back, and things quickly dried out. Passengers and crew worked together to dig out, rocking the lorry to and fro until it was free. Miles later, we went into a skid, and the top heavy vehicle rolled over with a thud, littering the desert with cargo and people. Everybody was shaken up. A few passengers had broken bones.

What happened next was eerie. After the initial clamor to see who was hurt and how badly, silence descended. There were no wailing sirens, no rush of emergency medical teams, no squeal of other cars braking to see what had happened. We were alone in the desert with our calamity. And we would remain so (mostly) for three days.

I had minor bumps and a badly bruised hip, but nothing serious. Other injuries, though not life-threatening, were serious and painful, and those who were hurt were made as comfortable as possible. Strangely, there was a lot of fussing over me. I was the guest in their country, and according to the teachings of Islam and the customs of Sudan, my well-being was a priority. I was given food, water, and comfort and reassured that our plight would soon be over. "Insha'Allah," they said: If Allah wills, all will be well. The understanding smiles increased in number and frequency. We built a fire and a makeshift camp. As the time passed, we began to look each other directly in the eye and communicate as best we could. The men told stories, which Kamal would translate for me, while the women combined beans, water, and oil to make the traditional meal of *foul*. Everything was shared. But when I tried to contribute my dates or nuts or bread, they were politely refused. I was the guest. I was embarrassed by so much attention, and also deeply touched.

No one seemed to be afraid. I took my cue from my companions and maintained my composure. When I asked Kamal how we would get out of this, he explained that we were on a regular trading route and the driver had assured him that other lorries would come soon. He did not seem totally convinced and was even a little contemptuous of the driver, as if he wanted it understood by all that the accommodations were not up to his usual standards. But after that first night, sure enough, another lorry came along heading west and took Kamal and me and the few with broken bones to the next tiny outpost, about two hours beyond. It consisted of two or three mud and grass huts for the herders and a well with drinking water. There were a few families living there or several generations of one large family. They made us as comfortable as they could while we waited for our lorry to be unloaded, righted, and loaded again so we could continue our journey.

My desire to be a citizen of the world had reached an unsettling turning point. I realized that no one at home knew where I was and that we had no plan for getting either back to Khartoum or on to El Fasher. We had the communal cache of food and enough water. And we had each other. As the days passed into nights and into days again, that seemed to be comfort for all of us. We slept and lounged on rude beds of hemp strung across short, rough sticks. We drank tea and told stories, my catching what I could and explaining what I could with my few Arabic phrases, with signs, with acting out, or with Kamal's help. The family elder was a thin, sturdy man whose wrinkled bronze skin and short gray beard were covered with a layer of sand dust, his bright brown eyes like pools of fresh water in the desert. He took an interest in me. His stories, comments, and questions were so constant that by the third morning Kamal became exhausted from translating. Limping from my bruised hip, I walked slowly with him to inspect his herd of goats and played little hand-slapping games with his grandchildren. He came to like me enough, apparently, that he offered me one of his daughters as a wife and part of the herd. (It was, I believe, a package deal, but I'm not certain.)

On the third afternoon, our lorry came lurching into the camp, its alignment clearly ajar, the cargo and other passengers piled high again on top. Without much pause, we gathered our bags, bid our farewells, helped the injured into the cab, and climbed back on board. At dusk, several hours out, trying to cross a deep *wadi* (a gully cut through the desert by flash floods), the lorry started to pitch over, and everyone who could leapt off to safety. The driver tried to rock the lorry back and forth by shifting between first gear and reverse, trying to get enough traction to climb up the far side of the *wadi*. Then the engine died. We spent another night in a makeshift camp, waiting for help.

By now we were a band of brothers and sisters. All were frustrated, but all saw the absurdity and some even the humor in our plight. Everyone realized that we were victims of events beyond our control but chose to cope not with panic or recrimination but with kindness and mutual support. The care shown the people with the most serious injuries was beautiful, the women simply stroking the hands of the injured and singing softly. It was so natural and so positive that it was not until long afterward that the danger of our circumstances settled on me. What emerged most forcefully was not fear but rather the sustained and triumphant grace of my companions. Even Kamal began to let his sense of his own superiority subside.

The next morning a lorry approached, headed east back to Khartoum. Our driver insisted that Kamal and I and those who were hurt should climb on top and ride back, and we reluctantly agreed. We rode much of the trip back in silence. I sensed that at some level Kamal was embarrassed about the experience, about how poorly he thought it reflected on his country and her people. But where he saw Third World disorder, I saw extraordinary generosity of every kind. At one point, we looked back from the horizon at each other at the very same moment and just started shaking our heads and laughing hysterically, releasing the tensions of the days before. Two or three days later, after we had found another lorry and refreshed our supplies, we set out again to El Fasher. After five long but uneventful days, driving by day and sleeping on the sand at night, we reached our destination.

There we found a room in a one-story concrete building that had an outside latrine and a cold-water shower. It was furnished with two of the hemp and wood beds that we had slept on while stranded in the Nubian. Nyala, on the other side of the Jebel Mara, the mountain that dominates Darfur, was a larger town but much the same. We divided our time between the two towns. We ate *foul* twice a day, sometimes with goat cheese and sometimes with camel's liver fried in strips and placed on top. Tomatoes and pungent onions in a little salad were a rare pleasure. During the Eid al-Fitr, the feast that marks the end of Ramadan, which was around Thanksgiving that year, we happened on a little camp across the mountain from Nyala and found a group of young men killing and frying whole chickens in a wok of boiling oil over an open wood fire. We sat under a spreading baobab tree for hours savoring the food and telling stories, my Arabic being pretty good by then. I did not know the word for *snake*, however, so I was a little slow to react when a small, deadly black mamba crawled under me and the men were yelling for me to move.

For months in Darfur, Kamal and I sat in the *souk*, befriending the young men who were the targets of the project, questioning them about what they knew about the employment training opportunities and what would make a difference in their decision to take advantage of them. Most of the time, Kamal asked the questions and I completed the surveys. After a little while, the pitfalls emerged, some so obvious as to make the original design of the project seem ridiculous. Using expensive power lathes in the classroom made little sense when power was unavailable for much of the day and when no such equipment would ever be seen at a Sudanese construction site. Offering classes during market hours was pointless when those same "unemployed" young men were out hustling, selling cigarettes or newspapers in the *souk* to earn enough to eat that day. Class sites too distant to get to from the *souk* . . . Well, you get the picture. For the project to work, we concluded, classes would have to be offered in or near the *souk*, after it closed, in skills needed and with tools used on a typical Sudanese construction site. The most effective incentive to bring the young men in was food.

After several months in Darfur, with a mixture of excitement and sadness Kamal and I boarded a retrofitted bus from China for the trip back to Khartoum. Many of the young boys and men I had met in the El Fasher *souk* came to see us off. We bounced along toward Khartoum, the bus packed, hot, and squalid, with my knees banging against the screws in the back of the metal seat in front of me until they bled. But I sensed I had been in the presence of something—in Darfur and across Africa—more meaningful than I could get from any book or class.

After my work in Sudan was finished, I traveled to Cameroon in West Africa, and then hitchhiked from there across Nigeria to Lagos, its capital, befriending strangers and spending the night in the homes of people I met along the way. Before the end of my fellowship year, I had trekked extensively around West Africa, through large cities and tiny villages, verdant bush and dusty desert. Benin,

Togo, Ghana, Mali, Niger were each so different—each with points of great pride, each with its own personality, its own aspirations and grudges.

I had never seen such poverty. It made my own experience growing up in Chicago seem small and insignificant. Most people lived in rudimentary shelters. Even in urban and highly developed Cairo, the poor crowded together as squatters on the roofs of the elegant apartment buildings along the Nile. Everything was put to use, every part of every animal, every part of every crop. And everything was shared. The generosity of material and spirit humbled me and changed me. I surrendered to it. Though I was sometimes painfully lonely as weeks turned into months without contact with home, I was repeatedly touched by the simple kindness of strangers. I met people on jitneys traveling between villages or on a plane, and through them I found a place to eat or lodging for the night. I felt as though I was being handed from one stranger to the next, hardly without interruption.

Even before my year was over, I knew I had stood in places that I could have never conjured on my own, and I had received what I had come for: a deeper understanding of how broken, impoverished, or otherwise challenging surroundings could not defeat the resourcefulness and generosity of people. I also received a daily lesson in compassion, a reminder of the transformative power of grace across all cultures, a template for how to treat those who speak, dress, or pray differently than I.

Those lessons have served me well in the increasingly rich gumbo that is America. In the years since, I have tried to bring those lessons into my practical life, rather than keeping them as just travel souvenirs. It is surprising how contrarian they feel in today's culture. In our age of high-decibel hate-mongering and attack ads gone viral, grace and generosity are sometimes viewed as quaint relics from a lost era. But that special giving of the spirit, which I first witnessed growing up and which was then so vividly reinforced in remote villages in Africa, sustains us all.

In my second campaign for governor, I was invited to meet with the Islamic American community and I agreed. Many members of the community were sensitive to how they had been shunned, even profiled, in the wake of the attacks of September 11, 2001, and they were hungry to have their pain acknowledged. Few politicians would accept an invitation to meet publicly, so it became a small sensation when I agreed. On the appointed day, more than a thousand faithful of all ages and stations in life crowded into the sanctuary at the Islamic Center in the Roxbury neighborhood of Boston. A score or more of the religious leaders sat behind me on the dais. TV cameras and a few nervous campaign staff watched every move. The air conditioner strained to keep us comfortable.

My remarks were limited. Most of the time was devoted to me listening to them, the stories of American citizens with Muslim surnames or foreign accents treated for that reason as suspects or outcasts, stories about their craving for understanding. I listened, remembering what grace had been shown me over thirty years before, what a difference it made not to be treated as an unwelcome stranger. Another candidate characterized the meeting as "pandering to terrorists." I viewed it as just the governor meeting with constituents or, even more, as one member of the community talking with others about matters that went far beyond politics. It was living a lesson.

Life is brimming with these opportunities, chances to expand your horizon and discover grace and generosity in unexpected places. Sometimes to see them you just need to try a different perspective.

Chapter 4

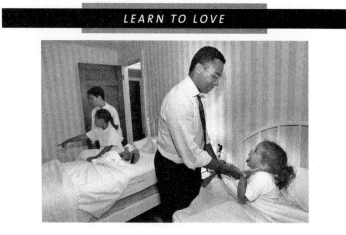

Reginald Lindsay grew up poor in segregated Birmingham, Alabama, but earned a place at Morehouse College in the 1960s, the first in his family to attend college. As a freshman, he and his classmates were invited to a rather formal dinner to meet the school's legendary president, Dr. Benjamin E. Mays. T-bone steak was served, a rare if not unheard-of indulgence for Reg, and he ate greedily. When he had eaten as much as he could with his knife and fork, he picked the bone up and, in his words, "commenced to gnaw at it."

Dr. Mays's wife, Sadie, was sitting nearby. An elegant, upright, Victorian force in her own right, she did not correct him outright. Instead, she offered him her own plate and said kindly, "Take mine, son."

She was teaching him how to behave, but she took care not to humiliate him. It was a moment of clarity wrapped in love and compassion, and Reg, who later graduated from Harvard Law School, became a partner at the law firm where I once worked, and served with great distinction as a federal district judge in Boston, never forgot it.

Love, I have learned, is like success itself: What matters most is not what you get but what you give. Selfless love is the most powerful. How you treat friends and family defines your own character and creates a ripple effect that can travel far and wide. That goodwill, that spirit of helping others, is the foundation of any community. It unifies and inspires. Sustaining loving friendships can test your patience and exhaust your resources, and "tough love" is sometimes required. But the most personal connections are sacred.

As a husband, father, and member of a community, I strive to honor those closest to me with love and respect and to create a home that is a haven. I want our house to feel to others the way the homes of A. O. and Aubrey Smith and June Elam felt to me. Some days, I believe I've reached those ideals; other times, I've been an abject failure. But the opportunity to make a difference in the lives of the people you care about most is a blessing itself. I had to learn to love that way, to understand both what you get from it and what you give to it. My wife, Diane, has taught me more about that than anyone.

After I graduated from Harvard Law School in 1982, I headed off for Los Angeles to clerk for Stephen Reinhardt, a recently appointed judge on the United States Court of Appeals for the Ninth Circuit. Judge Reinhardt was a gruff, rumpled, often surly, sometimes high-handed man who chewed off the ends of his pencils while he worked and could not even make coffee on his own. He was also brilliant, with a deep sense of justice and powers of concentration that I had never seen before. Clerking for him was a challenge because he tested and reexamined every aspect of every case, trying to get it right, and he required that his clerks be just as assiduous.

I made my way in this new job and new city and ever so slowly began to make some friends. One of the outgoing clerks was a delightful old soul named Robert Hubbell, who had recently married a generous, good-humored firecracker named Jill. They invited me to dinner with a friend of theirs, Debbie Barak-Milgrom, whom Rob had known in law school. Not long thereafter, the Hubbells and Debbie invited me to a Halloween party and insisted that I dress in costume. I reluctantly agreed.

I wore a full-length caftan from Nigeria and no shoes, smeared war paint across my face, and carried a Masai spear. I thought I looked pretty good until I walked into the party and realized that I was the only one in costume. The joke was on me. Little did I know that the surprises were just beginning.

The entire party was an elaborate scheme for me to meet Diane—to engineer a chance encounter—and I was the only one out of the loop. Debbie was Diane's close friend, and she thought Diane and I were meant for each other. However, my clerkship was for only one year; I was then heading to San Francisco to join a big downtown law firm. So Debbie, moving quickly, helped arrange the Halloween party. Diane knew why she was there and had been told all about me, including that my time in Los Angeles was limited. Everyone else knew the purpose of the party as well. I, on the other hand, dressed as a mock African warrior, was blissfully ignorant.

The light finally dawned during the pumpkin carving contest, when Diane and I were paired. The prize was a single bottle of champagne, "to be drunk," according to the hosts, "at some private time." We won, of course, but the contest was shamelessly rigged. We could have stabbed the pumpkin with my Masai spear and won.

I can't deny that I was delighted by my good fortune—how often are you set up with a beautiful, educated, friendly woman, smartly attired in a black silk pantsuit and pearl earrings—but I was also shy and a little embarrassed by my appearance. I didn't ignore Diane, but I was too timid to pay her any special attention. When the party finally wrapped up, we were at the door and Diane had our bottle of champagne. I guess she was getting impatient.

"Listen," she told me, "I'm going to take this bottle, and maybe one day I'll call you and we can share it."

"Sure," I said, "but I've got a better one at home."

I was shy, not clueless.

I got Diane's work number and called after a few weeks of screwing up my nerve. We got together for lunch at a Japanese restaurant. I was nervous and clumsy, chattering on about myself and getting precious little information about her. But my favorable first impressions were all confirmed: She was bright, a wonderful listener, serious, warm, and down to earth. She drove me back to the courthouse on her way to another appointment. As she let me out, I thought it was going well enough to ask her out for a real date.

"That was fun," I said. "When can I see you again?"

"You name it," she told me. Okay, breathe. She's interested.

"How about Saturday?" I asked eagerly. "We can go hiking."

"Saturday's not good for me. I'm moving."

"Great, I'd be happy to help," I lied, thinking that's as good a way as any to get to know each other.

Diane then looked straight at me, puzzled. "I don't think my husband would understand that."

"Your what?" She wasn't wearing a ring, and I never imagined that she was married.

"My husband."

"You're married?"

"Yes, but I'm moving out on Saturday."

Diane was stunned as well. She thought that I had been told about her circumstances, just as she had been fully briefed about mine. She was separating from her husband for the third and final time, preparing for a divorce. It was a tense moment all around. Diane later said that I had a look of disgust on my face. But I was more nonplussed than anything else. I had moved to California to start fresh, but this was a little too fresh for me. I would never date a woman who was married or at least still with her husband. Diane realized I had no idea that her marriage was long dead. She worried that I thought of her as a loose woman, out flirting while she had other commitments at home.

I got out of the car quickly. Neither of us knew quite what to say.

"Why don't you call me when you're free," I said. She was silent and nearly in tears.

That Saturday afternoon, my telephone rang. It was Diane; she had moved into a condo.

"I'm free," she said.

The next day we took a long hike together in the Santa Monica Mountains—with two other clerks. In fact, for the first several dates I always asked another couple or friend along. I just didn't know the right thing to do, how to rec-

oncile my attraction to this remarkable woman with knowing that she was married. Finally, Diane insisted that the
two of us have a date alone. Someone had recommended a
jazz club to her. The music and the food were both dread-
ful, but we finally started to open up to each other. In the
coming weeks, over dinners of red snapper at a beachside
café we came to like or late suppers after work at a French
bistro not far from the site of that fateful Halloween party,
Diane described the events that led to her unhappy and
even threatening marriage. I listened with both sympathy
and shock.

Diane had been raised in New York. Her mother, the
daughter of West Indian immigrants, was a schoolteacher
who also did the cooking, cleaning, washing, and other
household chores with a sense of wifely duty and determination. Her father, a master electrician and former navy
man, was a model of precision and rectitude, a stickler for
detail, and a strict disciplinarian. Her early years in Brooklyn and Queens were, in some ways, similar to mine. Her
family lived with her grandparents and extended family.
Her parents loved her though her mother was rarely out-
wardly affectionate. Diane was shy and diligent, a book-
worm who found her greatest fulfillment in the classroom.

She was also painfully self-conscious. One morning
about three weeks into her second-grade year, she was suddenly advanced to the third grade because she was so far
ahead of her second-grade peers. Petite and uncomfortable,
Diane was escorted by the principal and introduced to her

new class. As a gesture of welcome, she was invited to lead the class in the "morning exercises"—the daily recitation of the Pledge of Allegiance and singing of the national anthem. "Morning exercises" were unfamiliar to second graders, however, so Diane misinterpreted the invitation and started doing jumping jacks in front of the class. Even the teacher broke down in hysterics. Diane ran from the classroom, mortified. She would not return until her father brought her the next day.

Only sixteen when she graduated from high school, her parents forbade her from going to college outside the New York City public university system—or living away from home, for that matter—so she enrolled at Queens College of the City University of New York and studied early childhood education. She graduated with honors when she was twenty.

Diane found her affirmation and self-worth by teaching kindergarten and third grade in the New York City public schools. Because she was the junior teacher, she got the toughest classrooms, where the kids had little support at home. She poured herself into her job, but her position was eliminated during New York City's fiscal crisis in the late 1970s, and that layoff still left a painful expression on her face. She also occasionally worked summers at an advertising agency, in human resources. There, she met Bill Whiting, an advertising rep for a magazine. Fifteen years older than Diane, he was a real charmer, taking her to elegant lunches and dinners, flattering her, and paying her a kind of attention that was new to her. He validated her beauty and desirability in ways that no one else had before. Diane was both thrilled and enchanted. Before too long, and over the muted disapproval of her parents, she agreed to marry him.

Newly married and with her job in New York gone, Diane and Bill decided to move to Los Angeles and make a new start. It was a brave move for Diane, going so far from her extended family and friends, though she felt ready to leave the nest and was encouraged by her husband to do so. She enrolled in Loyola Law School, where she blossomed. Focusing on labor and employment law, she realized—perhaps for the first time—how much she was capable of. She excelled at law school, won awards, and, upon graduating, landed a position at one of the city's most prestigious law firms.

Just as she was discovering her talents as a lawyer, Diane was also discovering that Bill was a fraud. Many of the things he had told her turned out to be false. His college degree did not exist. His nest egg was empty. He had said he was close to his two children from previous relationships, but it turned out that he was estranged from them both.

With a lot of coaxing, Diane described to me, sometimes in a barely audible voice, how he became increasingly argumentative, disparaging, demanding, and verbally hostile. He humiliated her publicly, belittled her in front of friends, and slowly destroyed her self-confidence. Despite her academic and professional accomplishments, Diane was unwilling to assert herself at home. She had learned, growing up with her own parents, that women were supposed to be supportive, passive.

Bullied relentlessly and with no instinct to fight back, Diane became a victim to her deepest fears about her own worth. Here was this poised, downtown lawyer on the rise in professional circles, admired and relied on by the senior partners, who was barely holding it together under the surface. People are so much more than they seem, I thought. The shame she felt poured out with each new layer of her story. So did the fear. And with good reason.

One night, she told me, she came home late from the office with work still to do. Bill was waiting for her to make his dinner. She said she had to prepare for an arbitration hearing the following day, so he would have to fix his own dinner. She sat down at the kitchen table and began her work when he took out a gun and pointed it at her. She had not even known he owned a gun.

"You're going to cook me dinner," he said threateningly.

Unnerved, Diane cooked him pasta while he drank heavily. Once he had eaten and passed out, she took the gun, wrapped it in a towel, and dropped it off at a friend's house. When Bill awoke the next morning, he flew into a rage, pushed Diane up against a wall, and grabbed her around the neck. A month or so later, he got another gun. He became increasingly abusive, physically and psychologically. He pointed his loaded gun at her again and sexually assaulted her.

Diane soon left Bill, but not for long. She had come from a family and custom where marriage was sacred and divorce carried shame. Walking away wasn't easy, but staying away was even harder. After Bill apologized and promised to change his ways, Diane returned. The pattern repeated itself, and she left and returned a second time. They tried couples counseling, but, breaking from professional protocol, the therapist told Diane privately to get out of her marriage.

By then, Diane was afraid to leave—she feared for her life. It was obvious to me that she felt under siege, fragile, defenseless. She still functioned at a high level in her law practice, but outside work, her self-esteem lay in shambles. Bill had redefined who she was and made her feel as if she were the ugliest, most unworthy person in the world. She could not envision her life beyond surviving her immediate despair, and she had to fight the scourge of depression—the sleepless nights, the loss of appetite, the draining of all life's pleasures—each day.

Her personal trauma was not evident at the Halloween party. She glided around the room, talked easily with guests, and laughed at my lame jokes. In retrospect, she was a supreme example of the way people lock their secrets away so deeply, buried beneath layers of shame. Diane had been married for six mostly miserable years, and Debbie— one of the few people in whom she confided—had just about prevailed on her to leave Bill once and for all, even helping to arrange another place for her to live. Now Debbie was arranging a new love life.

In addition to seeing a beautiful, capable woman, I sensed there was something deep underneath: a tender heart, a beautiful soul. Our courtship became a slow journey of sharing and of gradually gaining trust. Maybe falling in love is always like that. But instead of falling for perfection, for an idealized version of what romance should be, I was learning to look past flaws, real and perceived, past the deep apprehensions that Diane brought to the relationship. At some level, Diane was reassured that I wanted to spend time with her. It contradicted all of the negativity and self-doubt that her husband had filled her with. I thought she was remarkable and said so. Slowly, she began to believe me. It is also true that I was learning to love in a more mature way, not with all the sweet-sounding harps and addled sighs and sentimental valentines, but in the slow, intimate, unconditional way that lasts. Each of us made the other better.

Bill did not go quietly. Diane continued to believe that he was going to try to kill her. Though he did not know where she lived, he knew where she worked, and he stalked her there. Every receptionist on every floor in her building had his photograph and would call security when he showed up. She felt safe in her office and with me, but hardly any-where else.

I was eager for her sake and the sake of our future to-gether for her to make the divorce final once and for all. Ironically, on a weekend getaway to San Francisco, it was Diane who asked if we should take our relationship to the proverbial "next level." I told her candidly that it was hard to know where it could go until her marriage was resolved.

Diane finally hired a lawyer to draw up divorce papers, but she did not want the Los Angeles County sheriff to serve them formally because she feared that Bill would be even more provoked to seek retribution. So she kept the papers in her purse and hoped to find the right time to de-liver them herself. Her hand was forced when some joint financial matter came up. She reluctantly called him at his office at the *Los Angeles Times,* where he was an advertis-ing rep, and spoke to his assistant, who didn't even know that he had separated from his wife.

The assistant said that Bill was in the hospital, hav-ing a medical procedure. Perfect, she ruefully thought. Assuming that he'd be in no position to hurt her, Diane decided this would be the time to give him the divorce papers. At the hospital, however, a doctor said that he had operated on Bill to remove hemorrhoids but had then dis-covered that Bill had advanced leukemia. He had six to nine months to live. When Diane saw Bill, he asked her to come home and take care of him. She could not do that, she told him—nor could she bring herself to serve him with the divorce papers.

Diane called me from the hospital, her voice shaking, and I met her back at my apartment. She was visibly upset as she explained that she felt sorry for Bill and trapped by his illness. She was stung by guilt but also confused. I cooked her dinner and spent the night trying to comfort her, trying to figure out a way forward for us both.

Events took another bizarre turn a few weeks later when Bill's disease went into remission. Once the hospital released him, Diane was really petrified. If he thinks he's dying, she thought, maybe he'll want to take me with him. I was soon heading to San Francisco for my next job, and we didn't know what our next move should be.

The following spring, when we were both working in her office, a senior partner dropped by and asked Diane to move to New York to help open the firm's new office in Manhattan. It was a huge vote of confidence, and she came into the empty office I was using to tell me the news. I was thrilled for her—but baffled when she told me she had turned it down. It would not only be a great professional opportunity and would reunite her with her family, but it would also put her at a safer distance from Bill.

"What's the real reason you're not going?" I asked.

"The real reason," she said, "is that I would love to have a future with you, and there's a better chance of that with you in San Francisco and me in Los Angeles than with you in San Francisco and me in New York."

"Well," I said without hesitating, "what if I went to New York, too?"

"Then I would go in a heartbeat."

"Then I'll go to New York."

And that was that. Without ever really saying as much, we were moving to New York together. She told her law firm that she would accept the assignment and move. I told my San Francisco law firm about my change of heart. With the help of Jim Vorenberg, my beloved college and law school mentor, I ended up with an even better opportunity in New York, working as a staff attorney at the NAACP Legal Defense and Educational Fund. In many ways, it was my dream job.

Just as we were moving, Diane filed the divorce papers with the Los Angeles County sheriff, who served Bill. We made our engagement formal and public. Diane still feared for her safety; even uncontested divorces require a waiting period, so several months had to pass, which they did fortunately without incident. We made a smooth if hasty move to New York. In a fateful visit, Diane told her parents all at once about divorcing Bill, her plans to marry me, her move home to New York, and the house we were buying together in Brooklyn. They took it all in stride, and her anxieties gradually subsided. Finally, on Valentine's Day 1984, the divorce was made final. Two days later, Bill succumbed to his leukemia. We were married later that spring.

Diane gives me credit for helping her out of a dark

phase of her life, but in truth, I got as much out of those early experiences as I gave. I had had girlfriends before, some serious, with all the usual highs and lows. I had never been involved with anyone as deeply as I was with Diane, however, or who was in as complex a situation. Fresh out of law school, with my whole professional life ahead of me and still trying to find my way, I didn't really want more complications. But there was a lesson here in unselfishness, a reminder that deeper love is less self-involved. My giving became a salve to Diane's wounded spirit, but once her self-confidence was restored, she gave back abundantly. Our marriage has now held strong through many personal and professional changes, and I believe our one constant has been our ability to give and receive selfless love.

I had learned from teachers and mentors how to love openly, generously, and conspicuously. I've also tried to impart high standards and accountability, which is its own expression of love. As our daughters arrived—Sarah in 1985 and Katherine in 1989—I tried to parent in that same fashion. Of course, I say that now. At the beginning, I was mainly a soft touch.

When Sarah was an infant, one of the first things she learned was how to kiss her dad. Good-morning kisses, good-bye and welcome-home kisses, good-night kisses— we grabbed every opportunity. We were (and are) a very tactile family, and I took special delight in the girls' plump little lips and the way they would hold hands by tightly gripping just a finger or two. Even as we were working hard to raise our family, though, I was mindful of how important it was for Diane and me to maintain our own relationship. So when Sarah was not quite two, I prevailed on Diane to take a short vacation alone with me to Bermuda. She was reluctant to leave Sarah, but I pestered relentlessly until she agreed. Diane's sister, Lynn, came up from Atlanta to collect Sarah for the few days we were away. At the appointed time, we were all ready to depart at Logan airport, Lynn with Sarah to Atlanta and Diane and I to Bermuda. I handed Sarah to her beloved aunt and said good-bye. When she reached back to me from Lynn's embrace, I burst into tears. We were well over the Atlantic before I composed myself. Diane still gets a good laugh out of that.

I won't claim that our daughters had typical childhoods. As well as providing emotional riches, Diane and I were learning as young downtown lawyers and business executives to navigate a new world of privilege and even occasional luxury, and the girls came along for the ride. We traveled all over the country and much of the world together. There were summer camps and riding lessons and dance recitals and town soccer, a hilarious affair where all the six- and seven-year-olds chase the ball without regard to zone or even who is on the same team. We took winter trips to the Caribbean with family friends, and the girls shook the hand of the president of the United States in the White House. They knew how to pronounce *concierge* and how to use one. At five or six, Sarah asked her aunt Lynn why there was no avocado in her salad.

When Katherine was in kindergarten, her class was studying the changes in the seasons—what happens in winter, spring, summer, and fall. Her homework assignment was to describe the four seasons to Mom and Dad. When she was ready, she proceeded to describe her several visits to the Four Seasons Hotel in Washington, D.C. "First you drive up and the doorman takes your car," she said.

"That's exactly right," said Diane gently. "But that's not what the teacher is asking."

In other ways, however, Sarah and Katherine were typical. Though they are close friends today and marvelously composed, witty young women, they bickered constantly as preteens. During one family visit to the Greenbrier in West Virginia, they harangued each other so bitterly in the dining room that Diane swore they would never come on a nice trip with us again. Once, driving on the Jamaicaway in Boston, they were so unbearably fussy in the backseat that I pulled over and put them both out on the side of the road and drove off. They were on to us, of course. When I circled the block to pick them up, confident that I had scared some sense into them, they were hiding in the bushes, purposely giving their parents the fright of their lives.

My work often took me away from home, and I readily acknowledge that Diane carried the parenting load far more than I in those years. I often took tearful calls from one of the girls complaining about a setback or mishap or their mom, only to be followed by a similar call from Diane. While everyone knew what I was trying to do for us as a family, I still carry a lot of guilt about having been absent. Yet the girls know that I love them. I say it and show it often and randomly, and it sometimes embarrasses them when I do, but it's important to them and to me that they have no doubt. That was a hole that my surrogate parents helped to fill in me, and I have tried to ensure that my own children never feel that absence. I've also tried to provide the girls with a love that reinforces their own self-worth.

Katherine, for example, once asked me to take her to a 50 Cent concert. I knew she was a big fan of the infamous rapper, whose real name is Curtis Jackson, but didn't know much about him or his music. I agreed, so I drove Katherine and three of her friends to New Hampshire for the event. Of course, taking a teenager to a rap concert does not actually mean attending it with them. In my case, it meant driving a few hours up to Nashua or Manchester and waiting in the bank parking lot across the street until it was over. Luckily, the producer was a friend of a friend, and I was invited, quietly and without Katherine's knowledge, to watch and wait from backstage.

When 50 Cent came on for his show, he wore two ammunition bandoliers across his bare, muscular chest. The sound effect between each number was the ratchet of a gun clip. To the screaming delight of a hall filled with hundreds of fifteen- and sixteen-year-old girls, he rapped about "bitches," "ho's," and violence. I got a glimpse of Katherine in the crowd, though she never saw me. Like the rest of the audience, she was completely beguiled.

Later, after we dropped her friends off, I asked Katherine about the concert. She said she had enjoyed it. I asked her if she knew what a *ho* was. She clearly knew, but she sighed, rolled her eyes, and said it was "just a word." I told her that it was important she know that she was neither a "bitch" nor a "ho," and that I never wanted her to accept being called that by anybody.

"You are a jewel," I said. "Nothing less."

Katherine scoffed at the time, but she got my message. I think her taste in music has "evolved" since then as well.

Years later, the summer after her nineteenth birthday, Katherine kept asking Diane and me when we would all be in the same place so that she could tell us something important. We were spending a weekend together at our home in western Massachusetts, preparing a picnic lunch, when she came into the kitchen and told us she was a lesbian. We both hugged her, told her we were there for her no matter what, and asked her to grab the mustard jar so we could get the picnic going. That was all she or we needed right then. The time for the endless questions would come in due course.

Alongside unconditional love, I've also tried to create expectations for our daughters. They know that I place a high value on decency, respect, and etiquette, all of which were emphasized in my youth. If one of their male friends came into the house with his hat on, I would politely ask him to remove it. We would not tolerate profanity or any other form of lazy speech—say what you really mean and feel without shortcuts, especially crude ones. We held our daughters accountable for the actions of their friends. Once, on the eve of her SAT exams, against strict instructions to stay home, prepare, and get to bed early, Sarah decided to go for a ride, and she gave her friend and study partner—who had no license and no driving experience—permission to back our Toyota SUV out of the carport. That was two strikes. Her friend proceeded to back the car into the front of the house, nearly knocking down the porch. Fortunately, no one was hurt. But that was strike three. The repairs to the house and car were costly, and I told Sarah that even though she wasn't behind the wheel, she would have to work all summer to pay off the bill. Diane thought I was being severe, but I felt it was an important lesson in responsibility and its consequences. Every two weeks, right after she got her paycheck, Sarah gave us a share until the bill was retired.

Despite such episodes, or maybe even because of them, our daughters know they are loved, and for me, being a father, like being a husband, is another lesson in selfless love. It's what you are no matter what else you are. Lately, it's finishing a press conference, a community meeting, or an important bill signing, then having one of the kids call when you are trudging home at 8:30 P.M. to ask, "What's for dinner?" It's feeling that same silly blend of pride and longing watching them graduate from college that you felt watching them graduate from preschool, children we have known, as my grandmother would say, since "before they knew themselves": children we have held and rocked to sleep, whom we have tickled and have gone swimming with and have taken to countless movies, whose heads we held while they threw up or brows we wiped when they had fevers, whom we read to and taught to ride bikes, whom we scolded and fussed at, who made us laugh at ourselves, whose greeting of "Hi, Dad" is enough to erase our every care and lighten our day, whose every smile makes us remember their first smile as clearly as if it were yesterday, whom we would walk through fire for, whom we have stayed awake worrying over long after they drifted off to sleep. Still do.

Diane and I have offered that same kind of parenting to other young people as well. Our home has always been something of a magnet. Given the number of children who have lived with us or have been central to our family over the years—sometimes we affectionately call them "the strays"—it is no small wonder that Diane feels we have rarely been alone. It's hardly surprising, though; it's how we both were raised. We have gotten as much out of it as we have given.

Not long after we were married and still living in Brooklyn, a friend from Massachusetts called to ask if her son, a budding dancer with the Boston Ballet School, could spend the summer with us while he studied with the School of American Ballet in New York. Of course we said yes, and Alex Brady arrived, all of fourteen or fifteen years old, trim and athletic, carrying a small duffel bag of belongings and a box of Cheerios. That summer turned into nearly three years as Alex's talent was recognized and SAB begged to keep him on and develop him. He went on to dance with the Miami Ballet and Twyla Tharp, but while he was with us, we were both learning how to live with a teenage boy. He was adventurous and wanted to explore the city and make friends. We tried to strike a balance between giving him room to experiment and keeping the eye on him that his parents expected. The call to come for him at the emergency room at St. Luke's Hospital was our worst nightmare. He had been stuck in the eye accidentally by the wooden sword of one of his friends during a medieval festival in Central Park. We arrived at the hospital to find a collection of his buddies dressed as serfs and knights sitting uncomfortably and conspicuously in the waiting room. Fortunately, it was a minor injury, and Alex recovered quickly.

My cousin Renae, Uncle Sonny's daughter, came to live with us for a while in Brooklyn, too, after the last of her immediate family passed away. She was not prepared for moving into the world of working adults. Diane took her shopping at Lord & Taylor for a suit for job interviews, something without sequins or her midriff showing. We practiced mock interviews and helped her write a résumé, and with her common sense and genuine warmth, she landed a job quickly. But when Diane came home from work one day to find her sitting in our front parlor with a guy she had just met on the subway, Diane had a firm talk with her about the proper way to introduce a new friend to the house: over Sunday supper, thank you very much, when we were both at home to greet him. Renae is now back in Chicago, married and raising a son of her own.

Soon after we moved to Milton in 1989, when Katherine was an infant, we became the host family for a Milton Academy freshman on scholarship from the South Bronx. Doug Chavez was an ABC student just as I had been nearly twenty years earlier, just as eager and earnest and just as clueless. Thin and small, he was carrying the bravado that he had used as protection at home, hoping it would do the same for him now. It all felt so familiar to me. Our responsibility was to befriend him, have him to supper a few times, and be a resource to answer questions if he needed us. We had a regular early supper on Sundays for our family and all comers. Doug came once and, in many ways, never left. He brought with him his rich Colombian-American heritage, his complicated family history, his hip-hop dance steps, his aspirations, and his friends whenever we invited him for Sunday supper or a family gathering. He had an opportunity to take a semester abroad in Spain, but it required that he offer his Spanish counterpart a place in his own home for a subsequent semester. We took in the exchange student as well. Doug became part of our family.

Doug had plenty to learn. Diane once heard him berating a girlfriend during an argument on the phone at our house. This was especially troubling because Doug had told us about his father's abusive behavior toward Doug's mother. He had no idea, of course, of Diane's own history. She went over to Doug in the middle of the call, hung up the phone in midsentence, and told him that that kind of language and treatment toward anyone, especially a woman, was unacceptable. He listened, and she made him a better man. Doug went on to graduate from the University of Pennsylvania and worked in marketing in New York. When I started my first campaign for governor, he left his job and moved back in with us for nearly two years to work on the campaign. Of course he remains in our lives today.

Though Diane and I loved having a full house, it sometimes took a toll. Shortly after Sarah was born, both my mother and father were living with us in Brooklyn for a time. (For various reasons, they both needed a place to stay.) We already had Alex with us. A colleague from work was going through a nasty divorce and was living with us, too, and his girlfriend visited for a time as well. Then our two golden retrievers had nine puppies the week before Sarah was born.

For some strange reason, everyone seemed to wait for Diane and me to get home from a full day's work to arrange meals and serve them. The dogs as well. This got old, especially for Diane. We lived in a wonderful, old, four-story row house, with the kitchen and dining room on the ground floor and Sarah in a bassinet in our bedroom on the third, and we managed this arrangement with a baby monitor we kept in the kitchen and regular trips upstairs. Sarah was colicky, so we were in the midst of that classic new parents' debate about how long to let her cry at night before going to her. We were exhausted, and one evening it all bubbled over when we came in from work to find everyone, once again, waiting for us to organize dinner. When we heard the baby start to cry on the monitor, I could see the tension rise in Diane's shoulders. We waited to see whether the let-her-cry school of thought (mine) or the rush-to-her-side view (hers) would prevail. Diane threw down her spoon and mixing bowl after a few minutes and rushed up the stairs. I thought it best to follow her.

When I reached our room on the third floor, I found the bassinet empty and Diane sprawled out on the bed, exasperated. Sarah was gone. My mother had come down from her room on the fourth floor to get the baby by the time Diane had reached our room, and she had had it.

"I can't stand having all these people around anymore," Diane ranted. "No one lifts a finger to help. We work all day and come home to them just sitting around and waiting for us to serve them, and I can't even comfort my own daughter without your mother intervening!"

She went on for a few minutes while I stood there nodding pathetically and feeling responsible. Then I pointed to the baby monitor, which was broadcasting her frustration to the kitchen full of houseguests. Diane's shocked expression is still one of my funniest memories.

"But we love all these people," she finally said to the monitor. After a few minutes in which we got our game faces on, we descended again to the kitchen; no one said a word, and everyone pitched in heartily. Most of our houseguests moved on not long thereafter.

Over the years, we've opened our doors to these and many other people who were hungry for company, attention, and affection. Growing up, I know that I too longed for these things; to give and to receive. I saw what happened with my own parents. While they were loving in their own way, their inability to express it to Rhonda and me not only withheld something from us but hurt them. Giving love freely is enriching for both the giver and the recipient. As a child, the love I did receive strengthened my foundations. As an adult, it makes me feel like I have value in the world.

When we have dinner parties, I like to go around the table and say something about each guest and our special connection to him or her. In addition to being a good icebreaker, it gives me a chance to testify publicly about the value we place on our friendships. Often, others at the table will follow my lead and describe how the other guests have contributed to their lives. It is like a snowball of goodwill. I think it catches everyone by surprise when we say aloud that we appreciate their presence in our lives.

Ironically, however essential it may be for our own souls to show that love, we often don't do so until it's too late. That came to mind when I visited an old friend, Morgan Mead, whom I had first met at Squam Lake as a teenager through Will Speers. I happened to catch Morgan after he had recently attended several family funerals. "You know," he said wistfully, "I'm giving all of these eulogies, and I'm getting pretty good at them."

"Morgan," I said, "that's fine, but you have to learn to tell people you love them before they die."

Chapter 5

SAVE A PLACE

When I was at Harvard, a fellow student who was a jazz aficionado figured out who my father was. I acknowledged the relationship and added gratuitously, "But he's a jerk." Jerome Culp, a black coal miner's son from Pennsylvania who was a resident graduate student tutor, took me aside afterward and encouraged me to respect my father publicly and keep our differences to myself. "One day you will find your way to each other," he said. "Save a place."

I was skeptical. The strained relationship between my father and me seemed irreparable, and the distance between my mother and me, for that matter, was wider than it should have been. But by the time Diane and I moved to Brooklyn and got married, my outlook had changed. When you're young, it's easier to hold grudges, I find, and allow conflicts to simmer. It almost comes naturally. But as an adult, you become more conscious of the passage and limits of time, and you realize that your ability to resolve personal differences is a sign of maturity. You come to understand that forgiveness is sometimes needed to heal ancient wounds. That's particularly true if the wound was inflicted by a parent.

My father—Laurdine Kenneth Patrick—had an unusual first name. As the story goes, my great-grandparents lived on a farm in Colorado Springs, some distance from their best friends, Laurence and Nadine. They promised their friends that they would name their first child Laurence if a boy, Nadine if a girl. After a series of miscarriages and stillbirths, my great-grandmother gave birth to a healthy son. Fearing he might be their only child, they invented the hybrid name Laurdine. Except on legal documents, my grandfather stopped using the name as soon as he was old enough to get away with it, preferring "Pat" instead. Growing up, we knew him only as Grandpa Pat. Still, he named his son, my father, Laurdine Jr. My father disliked the name as much as his father had and also used "Pat" professionally and socially. Even my sister and I called him Pat. But he passed "Laurdine" on to me as my middle name. There the tradition ends.

My father was skinny and tawny colored, with a black goatee, light brown eyes, and a bad left hip from a teenage football injury. He walked with a limp but otherwise never seemed to age: He credited health foods and herbal teas, long before they came into fashion. He thought that horehound tea, whose odor was comparable to that of a rotting carcass in the woods and which tasted like poison, cured anything. When I visited him as a kid, once I was given the tea for a cold. I concluded that the bad taste just made you forget what else ailed you. My father had a special charm, especially with women. There were many. Though I have no idea how he reconciled it with his black militancy, his girlfriends, for the most part, were white. It was one of many contradictions in a man I often found inscrutable.

My father inherited more than his first name from his father. Both were accomplished professional musicians. Grandpa Pat was a superb professional trumpeter who performed with and was close to Art Tatum, the great jazz pianist. Even so, my father had the real gift. As a student at

DuSable High School in Chicago in the 1940s, he studied saxophone and other reeds with the legendary instructor Walter Dyett. He was best known for baritone saxophone, for which he was routinely ranked in *Downbeat Magazine*. Over the years, I saw him perform every other saxophone and reed instrument, most wind instruments, the keyboard, and the bass as well—all with ease and confidence. An intense man with great powers of concentration, he was his most engaged, his most emotionally present, when riffing a jazz set.

He was also passionate about football. He knew the players, the teams, the standings, the history. When the televised games were blacked out in New York, he was known to drive his little VW bug to Connecticut, pull over to the side of the interstate, and plug a small portable set into the power jack to catch the game. Sometimes his music and his football collided. While my father was performing in the touring orchestra of the Broadway hit *Bubbling Brown Sugar*, the conductor chastised him for watching football on his portable television during performances. My father had a single earphone connected to the set to catch the game—and still never missed a cue.

My most vivid early memory of my father centers on the day he left. It was warm, and my mother was especially short with Rhonda and me that afternoon, which I attributed to the heat. I was oblivious to the mounting hostilities in our basement apartment. When my father came home, my parents started to argue, and their voices became loud

and abusive. Rhonda and I were uncomfortable and a little scared. As my mother, in tears, slumped in a chair, my
father stormed out of the apartment, up the stairs to the
street, and was gone. I chased after him, a four-year-old in
despair, while he strode away angrily, shouting at me, "Go
home! Go home! Go home!" About a block down, he lost
his patience, turned suddenly in a rage, and slapped me.
I sprawled out on the sidewalk, burning my palms on the
pavement. From that position, I watched him walk away.

Soon we moved in with Gram and Poppy, and life
more or less went on. I didn't know for many years why
my father left. All I knew was that he had moved to New
York with his band, the Sun Ra Arkestra. An avant-garde
ensemble full of virtuoso jazz artists, it had begun in Chicago in the 1950s and had an avid following. I met Sun Ra
once or twice. He was a little creepy, his music definitely
an acquired taste. It was not uncommon for him and his
band to perform in aluminum foil suits or with hats shaped
like planets. I met a diplomat once who told me that when
he was stationed in Lagos, Nigeria, Sun Ra came over
to perform at a Pan African music festival in an outdoor
arena. When the band appeared in their space costumes
and blasted their discordant tunes, mothers grabbed their
children and fled the stadium, crying, *"Juju, juju,"* the
equivalent of "black magic."

In New York, Pat Patrick fit in naturally with the
vibrant jazz scene and even became something of a phe-
nom. In addition to Sun Ra, he played and often recorded

with such jazz greats as Thelonious Monk, Duke Ellington, and Mongo Santamaria. Our mother told Rhonda and me that, no matter what, he was still our father and we should always love him. She insisted that we write to him. We didn't realize then that our mother's goal was to save the marriage, to make him miss us so much that he would set aside his music adventures and come home, which of course never happened. He occasionally wrote back. He occasionally sent some money. Sometimes he would call us on the telephone, which was a major event. Then there were the trips to New York when we got a little older.

For a time I felt somehow responsible for the breakup, as kids do. I also felt disappointment and anger and a certain amount of shame in having an absentee father, though that was not uncommon on the South Side. At least he wasn't in jail. He blew the sax, which other kids thought was cool.

My mother was brave but clearly devastated and maybe a little ashamed herself. In her youth, she had been known for her fine features and sassiness. She had clear, fair skin, auburn hair, a lithe, 5-foot-2 body, and a warm smile, dressed up in bright red lipstick. She liked to flirt. Old photographs show her sitting cross-legged and fetching at a jazz club or modeling for *Jet* magazine's "Beauty of the Week," wearing the fashions of the day, some borrowed from her job as a temporary sales clerk at the Saks Fifth Avenue on North Michigan Avenue.

But after my father left, the hardships on my mother

accumulated. She continued to flirt but with less conviction, sporadically dating an operative in the Young Democrats Club on the South Side. Her delay in getting a divorce doomed that would-be romance. Then her body turned on her. She developed discoid lupus, which attacks the skin, and was so irritated by it that she scratched deep, permanent scars on her face. For a young coquette who took so much pride in her beauty, these scars brought her overwhelming shame and despair. They disfigured her face, and struck at the core of her self-image and confidence. Her cherished good looks vanishing, her finances always on the brink, she started a long, slow slide into bitterness and depression.

Tensions between my parents continued on a low boil until I was twelve, when the pot finally exploded. I was right in the middle of it. Ironically, my father's love for music, which brought so much joy to so many, led to disaster.

My father tried to nurture my interest in music from a distance, which wasn't hard. In addition to Gram's spontaneous hymn singing around the house, my mother had a small collection of Billie Holiday and Sarah Vaughan albums she could play on my grandparents' hi-fi. Soul tunes poured from the AM stations on our transistors or from the 45s of Aretha Franklin, the Jackson 5, and later Marvin Gaye, whom we listened to in the phone-booth-sized spaces at the record store. Music was all around us. But just as my mother's urging us to write letters was as much about her needs as ours, my father's effort to interest me in music was also about him, not me.

When I was in middle school, he sent me a brochure for drum sets. At the time, I was taking lessons from a family friend, drumming on a set of practice pads and learning to read music, but I wasn't very diligent. The drums in the brochure, however, sure looked beautiful. I thought if I had my own and heard how real drums sounded, I would dedicate myself, practicing in the basement of our apartment building. I even circled the set that I liked. I sent my father letters and made phone calls, lobbying for my own instrument. This was, my mother quickly reminded me, a crazy idea—we barely had enough money for clothes and school supplies, and my father had studiously avoided contributing funds for our necessities. Besides, I would wake the dead, not to mention the neighbors, banging away in close quarters. The last thing we needed was a drum set.

The issue might have died, except my father made one of his rare visits to Chicago and came to take me out for the afternoon—just me and my father on an afternoon outing. I was excited. My mother knew what he was up to.

"Don't you get him a drum set," she warned. It was practically a dare.

We promptly went downtown to the drum store.

"Which one do you like?" my father asked.

I told him that Mom said I couldn't have one.

"Don't worry about your mother," he said. "You should have one."

I sensed this was not going to end well, but I could hardly turn my back on new drums and even picked out some premium Zildjian cymbals. The set had to be delivered, but I was permitted to take the snare drum with me, packed in a smooth black leather case with a brand-new pair of drumsticks. I rode home in silence with a mixture of excitement and dread. I kept thinking how best to play quietly to avoid disturbing the neighbors.

We walked into the vestibule, where my mother was waiting. When she saw my snare drum, the screaming began. She and my father just went at it, with my mother yelling that we needed money for food, not drums, and my father shouting that the boy should have his own instrument. Then my mother looked out the door and signaled to someone across the street. A man got out of his car, walked up the steps, and handed my father his divorce papers.

I never touched the snare drum again, and the rest of the set was never delivered.

And once the divorce was final, my father ignored the child support payments. It was an all-around disaster.

The summer before my senior year at Milton, Gram told me why my father had walked out so many years before. The day he left, she said, the phone rang in our apartment and my mother answered. The caller was a woman who asked for my father. When my mother said he wasn't home, the caller said, "Tell him our baby needs shoes," and hung up. The baby was my half-sister, LaShon, and my mother had known nothing about her or my father's infidelities.

Gram said that friction between my parents had been building for some time before then. My mother had had one or two abortions after I was born—at great risk to her health, because the procedure was still illegal then. She didn't believe my father could support additional children. When he learned what she had done, he flew into a rage. Their relationship never really recovered.

It is not surprising, in retrospect, that my visits with my father were never that joyful. He was invariably judgmental, as if he wanted to use our limited time together only to size me up. He would stand back and comment on my height, weight, haircut, clothing. He had very traditional views about what boys should do, with sports being high on the list. But I was not particularly athletic. My first real exposure to his beloved football was when our Cub Scout troop took a trip to a Chicago Bears game during a blizzard at Soldier Field, where games were played outside and the fans sat on concrete slabs. I was so frozen I could hardly walk by the time I got off the bus at home, and ever after I was lukewarm about the game, which probably disappointed him. He was also convinced that my mother's singular mission after their separation was to turn Rhonda and me against him, so whenever we were together he exhaustively catalogued her shortcomings as a wife and mother.

His obsession with race could also be wearing, and his visits to me at Milton were always perilous. Every word, every motion, oozed his disapproval. "Damn," he said when we drove around the neighborhood. "Everybody lives in a mansion around here." He met June Elam and approved of her race, but not of her swimming pool. She was too materialistic and "siddidy"—the scornful term blacks used to describe other blacks who were putting on airs. I was afraid to introduce my father to Will or A. O. Smith or any of my other new friends who were white. I wanted to keep him as far away from them as possible.

That could be avoided no longer on graduation day. It was a significant milestone, and I wanted to savor every moment. My mother, Rhonda, Gram, and Poppy drove out together from Chicago to share in it, the first such visit for all but my mom. We were, of course, conspicuously out of place. Most of the ladies wore classic tailored suits with gloves and hats. My grandmother, having just returned from a vacation on Waikiki (which was her and Poppy's first time on an airplane), wore a colorful Hawaiian muu-muu.

I had invited my father out of courtesy but admit to being relieved that he never replied, and I assumed he would not show up. Then, on the big day, while my family, friends, and I were having breakfast on the front lawn of Hallowell House, he appeared, grinning broadly if a little awkwardly. That familiar tension returned in an instant. I flashed back to the drum set debacle.

We made it through the graduation ceremony without a scene, but on our drive to June's house for dinner, the tension erupted. My mother, father, and I were together in the backseat of Poppy's car, my sister and grandmother in front next to him. Somebody said something, God only knows what, but it was enough to ignite the spark. In an instant, we had a full-blown conflagration going, my mother, father, and grandmother screaming at one another: assigning blame, settling old scores, reliving history. It was all about them and their issues. At a traffic light I just opened the car door, got out, and slammed it shut. I walked back to my dorm. They eventually found me there and reprimanded me for leaving them. But I didn't care. The day had been ruined.

Apart from that episode, my years at Milton had begun to mature me. I was beginning to feel like an adult and was ready to communicate with the adults around me on a different level. One day, during the summer after graduation, my mother and I decided to take a walk. We started at the beach on Lake Shore Drive, around 57th Street near the Museum of Science and Industry, and headed north toward downtown along Lake Michigan. It was a clear, unhurried summer day, and I started asking her about the things Gram had told me the summer before, about the breakup of her marriage, about the poverty she tried to hide from us. She did not stop me or try to shut off the conversation, which was her usual way with delicate matters. Instead, with calm candor, she described her disappointment with my father, the humiliation she felt at having to move in with her parents, the conflicts she had with her own mother, the indignity of poverty, the embarrassment about her scarred face. It poured out of her in measured, mature conversation unlike any I had ever had before with my mother. I think we were both surprised. I'm sure she had long thought that I was incapable of understanding her life and struggles. And I expected my curiosity to be met with her customary distance and emotional barricades. But we kept talking, each of us finally appreciating the other. She did not want pity, just understanding. We kept talking and walking—all the way downtown and back. We covered a lot of miles . . . and a lot of ground.

The terrain with my father proved more difficult.

The summer after my freshman year at Harvard, I was hired by a management training program at Chemical Bank on Wall Street. I initially stayed with a friend from Milton whose family lived in one of those opulent buildings on Fifth Avenue in which the elevator opens directly into the apartment. I had never seen that before. I had arranged for my own place with some other guys, but it fell through, so I had to ask my father for help. He was living in Queens with a black dancer named Marianne, to whom he was either married or about to be married. He told me I could sleep there until I figured out other housing arrangements. I ended up staying for the whole summer.

They lived in a one-bedroom flat in an apartment complex off Hillside Avenue, just blocks, as it turned out, from where Diane grew up. I slept on a pull-out sofa in the living room, between their bedroom and the bathroom. We could not avoid one another, nor could we connect. My father disdained Harvard as much as he had Milton, and he continued to openly disapprove of the man I was becoming. It did not help that every day, to his amusement or disbelief, I dressed in a business suit, a tie, and "big boy shoes." I read the *New York Times* and the *Wall Street Journal* on the E train to Lower Manhattan, smack in the heart of the global financial district, and I walked confidently through the hushed corridors of the Chemical Bank headquarters.

The training program itself was mostly for minority students, and I became friends with other students from Princeton and Barnard. We were well paid for a summer job. We dined at nice restaurants, ordered drinks at the finest bars, and attended Broadway plays and the ballet. We were pretending to be part of the establishment—trying it on, so to speak, and having fun—but it was all just too much for my father. Our lifestyle was the final surrender to capitalism, in his view, to the white power structure, to the institutions that had oppressed blacks forever. This was what Milton, Harvard—and my mother—had begot.

The other thing going on that summer, I suspect, was a concerted effort by me to avoid spending much time with my father. We had a tiresome pattern of long, uncomfortable silences, and I was in no hurry to seek out more of that. Toward the end of the summer, however, my father asked me directly to go for a drive so we could talk. He needed to get something off his chest. We pulled over just off the Grand Central Parkway, near Flushing Meadows, where Rhonda and I had spent such a wondrous time with him at the World's Fair when we were kids. My father pulled out note cards on which he had collected his points and began speaking—a steady, passionate stream of frustration, accusation, and invective. He told me all the ways in which my mother had failed as a mother, why she had driven him away, why she had betrayed my black identity, and on and on. I found those notes in his effects after he died. They still sizzle.

I really had no choice but to sit there and take it. He spoke for nearly two hours, raising his voice to overcome the roar of traffic passing by the open windows and to convey his pent-up emotion. Years of fury and regret gushed out of him. When he was finally spent, I surprised both him and myself by being calm. I told him quietly that I certainly missed having him in my life as a young boy but did not blame him for not being there, and that my mother's urging of him to see Rhonda and me was the only reason he knew us at all. If we were going to have a relationship, I said, it would have to be about the future, not the past.

"I haven't made any judgments against you," I said. "I don't even know you. The fact that I'm making other choices is not about you." So let's move on.

He was stunned that I did not fight back on his terms, yet stood my ground. We drove back to his apartment in silence. Nothing had been settled, but it was the beginning of a process in which I would try to forgive him for the hurt his long absence had caused us, and he would try to accept me for the man I was becoming. I would save a place.

After our long walk that summer day, my mother and I became much closer. We began to accept each other as adults, as friends. During the year I spent in Africa after graduating from Harvard, she even came to visit. It was an adventure all its own.

The villages where I lived in Sudan had no postal or phone service, so my mail was held for me at the main post office in the capital. Returning there from Darfur was the end of a long, lonely spell without contact from home. What a treat awaited in December when I visited the dusty, colonial post office in Khartoum to find piles of unopened mail. I needed a large bag to haul them away. I put the letters in chronological order and worked my way through them over several days. My friends' sprawling lives, their milestones and their crises, were neatly compressed and resolved in one or two readings.

When I eventually reached one of the letters from my mother, dated sometime in early November, she wrote that she had saved her money so she could come see me, and I should meet her in Nairobi, Kenya, for Christmas. Since

I had been anticipating the strangeness of my first Christmas away from home alone in a foreign environment, I felt a surge of excitement. I was touched by the gesture, too, since Mom had never traveled overseas before.

I quickly realized, however, that the date she had set for our rendezvous was only two days away. Her letter was weeks old by then, and she had, of course, received no reply from me that I would meet her. Communicating with her quickly was impossible. In those days, phone service in Khartoum was spotty at best. Even when it worked, an international call was expensive, required making a reservation at the phone company headquarters downtown, and was likely to be interrupted anyway. Sending a fax was impossible for ordinary people. There was no such thing as e-mail, cell phones, or text messaging. According to her letter, my mother would be flying into Nairobi, but she made no mention of airline, flight number, or where she would be staying. Just "meet me in Nairobi."

I hustled down there by effectively hitching a midnight ride on a British Airways flight out of Khartoum. Luckily, my friend Kamal, with whom I had worked those many months out in Darfur, had a friend who worked for the airline. The friend sold me a deeply discounted ticket and got me on the already full flight when it stopped in Khartoum at midnight en route to Addis Ababa and Nairobi. I'm not sure how he did it. All I know is that a groggy and bewildered European businessman was escorted off the plane onto the empty tarmac just before I was told to grab my big backpack and hustle aboard to a seat in the back. The ways of Africa are sometimes mysterious!

I landed in Nairobi amid uncertainty and confusion. The city is on the equator and is warm and tropical even in December. The airport terminal itself was a big open shed with no walls and a tile floor, with colorful birds gliding in and out, taxis milling along the curb on one side and an opaque glass barrier on the other, with sliding doors to admit arriving passengers. I found airline personnel and explained my dilemma. They were incredulous. There were no direct flights from Chicago, and I had no idea how she was connecting to Nairobi. The airlines, meanwhile, refused to give out any information about their flight manifests. So I simply met every international arrival—for a day and a half. Each time the door of the arrival lounge opened to disgorge passengers and closed again, I rode a cycle of anticipation and disappointment. I kept watching other people's reunions, a great cross section of the continent—white, black, Asian, businesspeople, farmers, families, and friends. But not my mother. It was warm during the day and cool at night, and I slept fitfully between flight arrivals on an uncomfortable plastic bench.

Then, improbably, there she was. She looked tired but cheerful, smaller than I remembered, wearing a flowery shirt and floppy white canvas hat. "I wasn't sure I would even see you here," she said, laughing. My exhaustion and frustration gave way to tears of relief. She wept as well.

I asked what she would have done had I not been

there. She said she had met a lovely Kenyan family on the plane, and they would have given her a place to stay. I had to admire her moxie—picking up from a tenement on the South Side of Chicago, flying to Nairobi, and thinking, I'll figure it out along the way.

We stayed for a few days in a small colonial guesthouse set in a garden, which served cold toast and tea for breakfast. The Kenyan staff would greet my mother warmly each morning with "*Jambo, Mamma,*" which means "Hello, madam" in Swahili. But my mom would reply with "Jumbo," which usually elicited peals of laughter. She couldn't quite get the hang of it. However, we were always treated well. Respect for elders is very important in Africa, and my traveling with my mother was quite endearing to the Kenyans. We organized a couple of safaris, though she could have lived without the lizards that invariably scuttled across the ceilings at night wherever we stayed, and when some critter came too close to our van in the game parks, she shrieked. We stayed in tented camps, dined on multicourse feasts of fresh soups and roast lamb or stewed Kudu at night, slept under the brightest stars, and listened to the sounds of elephants crashing through the bush or hyenas yelping just beyond the camp. We walked up Mount Kenya, not quite to the summit but to about 14,000 feet; my mother was a longtime smoker, so it was a struggle for her, but she persevered. We took an elegant overnight train to Mombasa, down by the sea, where the blend of African and Arabic influences made a spicy mix.

It was a wonderful visit. After many months on my own in Egypt and Sudan, I was accustomed by then to the rhythms of Africa and was at ease making my way, bargaining in the markets, eating the local foods, and sensing which chances to take and which to avoid. Like any first-time visitor to so foreign a place, my mom was always checking her passport and her travelers' checks to make sure all was in order. She had to rely on me more than either of us was used to. It was a new chapter in our relationship, and we both took to it.

She stayed for almost two weeks, and when she left, I felt a deep void. I couldn't believe she had traveled so far to see me. She had never been very good about showing affection or saying she loved me, but her unlikely trip spoke more eloquently than any word or gesture.

In the years immediately following the blowout with my father, our relationship slowly began to mend, and my time in Africa played a central role. He was always citing the Motherland and his ancient Egyptian roots and reminding me how much more advanced African civilizations were than those of Europe. He had traveled to Egypt, Nigeria, and elsewhere in Africa, and that continent's proud history stood in dramatic contrast, he believed, to the history of humiliation that blacks had suffered in America.

I wrote to him from Africa and described how rich and inspiring my experiences were, and this embossed my credentials with him. He stopped questioning whether I was black enough. It helped that my familiarity with African culture and history, given my time on the continent and my reading of African literature while there, was growing deeper than his. When I returned home for law school the following year, we checked in with each other more often, though I still didn't see very much of him, except on one memorable occasion.

The summer before my third year of law school, I worked at a law firm in Washington, D.C. I turned twenty-five that July, and on my birthday, my father happened to be playing in a local jazz club called Pigfoot and invited me to join him. I hadn't spent a birthday with him since I was three, but I agreed.

I arrived near the end of the first set, just before the break, and my father was playing the saxophone, jamming with a skilled quartet. I took my seat at a little table, and he nodded when he saw me come in. When they finished the number, he took the microphone and said to the crowd, "It's my son's birthday, and I want to play this next tune for him."

There was warm applause and an approving glance or two my way from other patrons. Then the place got quiet, and he played an old standard, "I Can't Get Started." There was no vocalist, but by then I had developed my own love for jazz, and I knew the words.

> *I've been around the world in a plane.*
> *I've started revolutions in Spain.*

The North Pole I've charted.
Still I can't get started with you.

He looked me straight in the eye while he played, long and soulfully, full of regret and longing all at once. I gazed right back at him, knowing what he was trying to say: Life is too short to go on like this; let's find a way to come together. No words were spoken, but the music gave us our own language. We communicated more in those few moments than we ever had before, and it was clear how much we both wanted simple understanding. We weren't quite there—when I graduated from law school, he did not attend the commencement—but we were moving closer, and it seemed my father never felt threatened by my choices again. I had saved a place, and so had he.

After law school, while I clerked for Judge Reinhardt in Los Angeles, Rhonda was living not far away in San Diego with her husband, Bernie, and their infant daughter. Grandpa Pat and various cousins on my dad's side lived nearby in Orange County, so family gatherings included my father. They were infrequent, but relaxed and pleasant. He was eager to be in California as much as possible, as if to make up for lost time with Rhonda and me. It worked because we were building a relationship on tomorrow rather than yesterday.

Diane, too, was instrumental in the efforts between my father and me. I had always been open with her about my disappointments in my father, his abandonment of his family, his failure to contribute to our upbringing, his breaking of my mother's heart. But, even before she met him, Diane also sensed my respect for his intelligence and his musical gifts and my longing to be closer.

Soon after Diane and I had settled into our home in Brooklyn, I noticed an ad in the *New York Times* saying my father would be playing with a small ensemble at a jazz club on the Upper West Side. I suggested we go. Diane was reluctant because she didn't want me to reach too close and be hurt again, but I insisted.

When we entered the small bar, with its smoky red walls and dim light, the trio was in the middle of a number. My father looked up immediately, stopped playing mid-note, and left the bandstand to come over and throw his arms around me. I returned the embrace, and soon we both had tears in our eyes. When I introduced him to Diane, he could not have been more gracious and charming. They became instant friends.

He became a frequent guest at our house, and Diane had an ease about his presence that allowed us to move forward. He adored her, and she always welcomed him into our home, invited him for dinner, and enjoyed his company. She gave us both space to move at a deliberate but comfortable speed. We talked about old times, but without the bitterness. He told me how his slapping me on the day he left was something he had regretted ever since. I said he could now let that go.

When Diane and I got married, my father organized his friends to play at our wedding. This ensured that we had not just good music but *any* music, as we lacked the funds for a band. My dad had a rousing good time playing background for Diane's father's singing. He even secretly taped our wedding and gave it to us as a special gift. Before the wedding, I worried about how my parents would behave with each other. They had not been together since that fateful encounter at my graduation from Milton. But they treated each other like old friends. Reconciliation seemed to be in everyone's heart.

My father took to staying with us in Brooklyn for long periods when he was between concert tours or on the outs with his girlfriend. Even when he wasn't living with us, he was part of our lives, and he was eager to play his part as father-in-law.

After we told him that Diane was pregnant and as the date approached, my father called every day to ask for any news. I kept assuring him I would call when there was something to report, but he kept checking in anyway. On the one day he missed his check-in, Sarah was born after a long and trying labor. I called and called for a couple of days thereafter but could never reach him. Then, the first day that Diane was feeling herself again, I went by her favorite Italian restaurant to pick up a special dinner to take to the hospital. Laden with the food and flowers and little gifts for her and the baby, I stood on a midtown corner trying to hail a cab. My father was then driving part-time a business tycoon's gray, stretch limousine, and he miraculously spotted me. He pulled up, told me to hop in the back, and asked me where I needed to go. There, from the backseat of a stranger's limousine in rush-hour traffic, I told him to take me to Lenox Hill Hospital, where I was going to have dinner with his new granddaughter.

The generational bonds were now secure. My dad continued to visit intermittently between concert tours overseas. By the time Katherine had grown into a sassy toddler, he would come to our house in Milton and dote on two precious little girls. He gave them fifes and little flutes and played the sax for them while they danced around our front hall, and he showed them the gentleness, attention, and love that I so craved in my own youth. Sarah and Katherine loved him in return, and my father reveled in it. How fitting that the finest gig of his life was that of grandfather.

My mom's life took a very different turn. Soon after Diane and I were married, my mother took ill and could no longer care for herself. After a long stay in the hospital, where the doctors could not determine the cause of her seizures and partial paralysis, she moved into a rehab facility in Chicago. When it seemed that there was no hope she would get better, we moved her in with us.

In some ways, her presence seemed natural for both Diane and me, having grown up in multigenerational households. But this arrangement required many sacrifices. In Brooklyn, my mom saw specialists who gave her medication that helped her regain her mobility, but her spirits suffered horribly, and her emotional decline wore everyone down. She helped when she could, especially when Katherine was born and we could not find a suitable sitter to manage both kids. But over time my mother seemed to resent her dependence on us, and perhaps even my relationship with Diane, who shouldered an even greater burden around the house. I'll forever be grateful to Diane for accommodating her. My mother did not always make it easy.

My mom lived with us for twenty years, and whatever her physical or emotional state, it was important to me that she always felt part of our family. In the 1990s, for example, when I was the assistant attorney general for civil rights, the *Los Angeles Times* wrote a profile on me and sent a photographer to our home for a family picture. Diane, Sarah, Katherine, and I were on the stairs, ready for the shot, when I noticed my mom sitting alone. I told her to get in the picture.

The photographer said, "No, I just want the family."

I don't know if he didn't want her because of her scarred face or—a more generous interpretation—because he wanted only my immediate family. But it didn't matter.

"My mom is part of this family," I said.

I knew how self-conscious she was, but I also understood how proud she was of me, Diane, and the girls, and how important it was for her to be included in this photograph. She came over, sat next to Sarah and Katherine, and smiled.

In the summer of 1993, while my father was visiting, Rhonda and I took a long walk with him and our kids on the Freedom Trail in Boston. It was a hot day, and we stopped for a cool drink and a bite to eat at an open-air restaurant at Faneuil Hall Marketplace. Suddenly the color drained from my father's face, his speech began to slur, and he collapsed in a seizure. The restaurant summoned an ambulance. The kids were frightened and upset, so I took them home while Rhonda rode with Pat to the hospital. He was diagnosed with leukemia. Not long after, he left New York and returned to his hometown of East Moline, Illinois, to be close to his mother and other family members. I didn't fully appreciate it then, but he was going home to die. Late that year, we were preparing to go on a cruise, and I got word before we boarded in Miami to call my father. From a pay phone in the Miami airport, I reached him at his hospital, still not fully understanding how grave his condition was. His voice was weak, unlike I had ever known it, but also eerily calm. He said frankly that he thought the end was near; he did not need me to come but just wanted to say good-bye. I told him that I loved him, and I meant it.

"I'm not quite ready to let go of you yet," I said.

I meant that, too. It was the last time we spoke.

It was my mother who called us ship to shore on New Year's Day to say my father had passed away. Her voice cracked. I sat for a long time alone on the deck, staring out at the tropical sea, trying to figure out how I felt. Sad. Regretful. Forgiving. Admiration for his total dedication to his art. Understanding how we muddle along, bumping into circumstance and opportunity and tragedy, but ultimately having faith in the people closest to us.

More than a full decade would pass before my mother became gravely ill with hepatitis and uterine cancer. In a life of many difficult moments and with so many reasons for regret, I believe she deserved all the tenderness and friendship that Diane and I, as well as my sister and her husband, could give her. Despite her often unfair treatment of Diane, in her final year it was frequently Diane who would feed and bathe her and keep her company. At the end, she was in the same nursing home where my grandmother had spent her last days, and she died there in January of 2005 on the day the *Boston Globe* reported that I would be a candidate for governor.

At the reception after my mother's memorial service, someone asked me what it felt like to be an orphan. Strangely, I felt as though I already knew the emotional distance that orphans must experience. But I also came to know the moral imperatives that every family confers on every member—to comfort and love, to support and encourage, to bless and forgive. Sometimes the last one is the hardest. It was for me, and I wish I had understood its importance sooner. But there is no statute of limitations on forgiveness. You need only save a place, and because I did, I found reconciliation in good time. That is comfort enough.

Chapter 6

FAITH IS HOW YOU LIVE

My mother did not care much for church. By the end of the week, she was bone tired from work and the weight of her misery. But my grandmother was a child of the South, and for her, church on Sunday was a must. She was an envied soloist for many years in her church and punctuated her days around the house with soulful hymns. Though she also cursed like a sailor, she quoted scripture often. There was no question in her mind that my sister and I would be raised in the church, and she insisted we go every Sunday.

Her means of enforcing this rule did not involve

threats of eternal damnation so much as the promise of a big country breakfast when we came home. In a household where her groceries were strictly segregated from my mother's and where my sister and I were always hungry, Sunday mornings (like holidays) were occasions for a common feast. And these were big country breakfasts, prepared in the traditions Gram had brought with her from Kentucky—eggs, sausage or scrapple, bacon, grits, homemade biscuits and gravy, fried apples in the fall, sometimes liver and onions. We awoke to the luscious smell of bacon frying. We could not partake, however, until after church. It was a bribe, pure and simple. And it worked.

The Cosmopolitan Community Church was just a block away, on 53rd and Wabash Avenue. It was an unusual black church for its time. The pastor was a woman. Dr. Mary Evans was humble, subdued, and elderly, with dull, limp gray hair and skin so fair she may have been white. The church seemed to be in decline. The pews were hardly ever full except on Easter Sunday. Today there is an updated sanctuary, with modern broadcast and sound systems and a band with an electric bass and drums. But in my childhood, services were held in a cool, dark space with wooden folding seats, a wheezing organ, and, behind the altar, a lighted cross. Services were quiet, even a tad boring, with little of the shouting or theatrics of many black churches. I was baptized there just before I went off to Milton Academy, wrapped in a white sheet, fully immersed in a big bathtub of warm water that appeared from behind a wine-colored velvet curtain. That was about as close as we came to drama at Cosmopolitan.

What I recall most vividly are the old ladies. They wore dresses whose bright colors had faded or tailored suits in shades of brown or gray that may once have fit. Some wore gloves, yellowed with time. They all wore hats—pillboxes, ovals, broad-brimmed, and those little numbers shaped like military caps or fedoras—with ribbons and pins and plumes. All the jewelry was costumed and dated but worn with pride. The ladies swept into the church with their grandchildren in tow and seated themselves with little ceremony, clutching their frayed King James Bibles, ready to get down to the business of worship. They nodded their approval during the sermon or when student achievements were acknowledged, fanned themselves when it was warm, and glared at fidgeting children.

Old ladies ran the place. When it was time to sing, they chose which hymns would best suit the pastor's message by humming the tunes until the organist caught on and caught up. The music rose from our pews, and the songs themselves—"Amazing Grace," "The Old Rugged Cross"—were haunting, reverent, and spiritual. At the end of nearly every service, one particular old woman who sat in front would sing "Blessed Assurance" with conviction, white spittle collecting at the corners of her mouth, and the others would join in. People always sang like they meant it. Their hymns lifted us to a higher plane—the common miracle of every black church I have ever visited. The overall tone was one of peaceful reflection, of true sanctuary. Once there, I inevitably forgot that I just wanted to earn the big breakfast back home.

I watched those old ladies and, more important, experienced them. I knew from overhearing my grandmother's gossip about the calamity in their own lives, yet I saw them encourage others when they themselves were suffering, when a child of their own was in trouble, when their own husband had lost his job, when their own spirit was in need of renewal. I got hugs when my good grades were announced, even when their own grandchildren had slipped into a gang. Their ability to love selflessly was constant and certain.

I have had so many blessings in my own life, so many improbable gifts, that I am long past questioning whether there is an invisible hand at work in my life. To me, God is real. But my years at Cosmopolitan, and the experience of those old ladies in hats, emphasized that faith is less about what you say you believe and more about how you live. I came to see those old ladies as embodiments of the faith we were taught. They showed me how to welcome and embrace all the people who walked into our church and into our lives, from whatever station. They meant "embrace" literally—a hug, a tactile expression of oneness and support.

Scripture itself is full of poetry about kindness and magnanimity, about the charge to care about and help your fellow man. In the words of the prophet Micah:

> He has shown you, O man, what is good; and what does the Lord require of you but to do justly, to love mercy, and to walk humbly with your God.

These truths are nondenominational. They can be found in the Koran and the Talmud as well as in the Bible. When Gordon Brown, the British prime minister, gave a speech at the Kennedy Library in Boston in 2008 on the strategic importance of foreign aid to poor countries, he described how all the major religions of the world have some version of the Golden Rule, that we treat others as we wish to be treated. Humanity cries out for this in every language on earth. Still, so little of our behavior, public or private, reflects what we all know to be true.

Some of these simple truths of faith traditions are lost in the pomp of organized religion. The pageantry of the Catholic mass or the rituals of Islamic prayer seem sometimes to overtake the message itself. Black ministers and white evangelical preachers, with their capes and dancing and speaking in tongues, sometimes let the showmanship and the fundraising crowd out the lesson of compassion in the text. Islamic "fundamentalists" obscure the gentleness of Islam and turn disenfranchised Middle Easterners into radicals who blame nonbelievers for all their troubles. It is hardly new in history to have religion used to justify oppression, hatred, or even violence. Still, it is jarring. More than once I have sat in a religious service and wondered what in the world the sermon's message had to do with the simple command to show justice, mercy, and humility in our lives.

But the old ladies of Cosmopolitan keep calling to me. It is probably thanks to them that social justice has been at the core of my professional life. Social justice is faith in action. Judaism summons a charge to all believers: *"Tikkun olam,"* to repair the world. The notion, as our friend Amy Gorin puts it, has come to mean to live life as if you bear some responsibility for improving the lot of others. *Tikkun olam* is a call to look beyond ourselves and to see our stake in one another. That is the essence of community. We do not have to save the entire world on our own, but we can each repair some small corner of it. Our responsibility is to try. That is what the old ladies of Cosmopolitan were trying to teach me, and their example has led me to some remarkable places.

I thought of law school as a way to express my commitment to social and economic justice—and also to make a buck. When I got there, it seemed that many more of my peers were focused on doing well than on doing good. I found kindred spirits at the Harvard Legal Aid Bureau, the oldest student-run legal aid clinic in the country. There, law students could handle civil cases for clients who couldn't afford lawyers. The work suddenly made real the abstractions of book learning.

In one early case, I represented the Jean-Pierres, a poor Haitian family with three small children living nearby, in Somerville. They were behind on their rent, the landlord had turned off their heat, and the family was using its oven to warm the house. They were about to be evicted. They were confused and vulnerable, and they needed help. Their English wasn't very good, my Creole was nonexistent, so we communicated in broken French. Haltingly, I learned about their struggles in Haiti and in Boston, their determination to make it in Massachusetts, their love for their family and America.

Their case was pending in the Somerville District Court before a notoriously difficult—and famously pro-landlord—judge. I was as nervous as the Jean-Pierres, so I prepared exhaustively. I filed my motions and counter-claims and won a stay of the family's eviction until trial. The case then went to trial, which was unheard of in a landlord-tenant dispute. I made my opening statement, presented my evidence, cross-examined witnesses, and argued that in Massachusetts, you can withhold your rent if the conditions of tenancy have been violated. I showed how the faulty appliances, sporadic utility service, poor insulation, and general unresponsiveness of the landlord were chronic and justified my clients' withholding the rent. We won, and the judge grudgingly ordered the largest payment to a tenant in the history of that court at the time. My clients never collected, but they remained in their home and stabilized their lives. I will never forget the look of relief on their faces and the pride they felt as immigrants in a system that would vindicate those who were most vulnerable. That, I felt, was why I was in law school—the secular extension of everything I had learned in church. And I was touched, during my first campaign for governor, when one of the daughters of the Jean-Pierres called after all those years to wish me well.

When I joined the NAACP Legal Defense Fund after my clerkship in Los Angeles, I was thrilled to have the opportunity to put social justice into action. The organization and its legal giants—Thurgood Marshall, Spotswood Robinson, and the man who hired me, Jack Greenberg—cast a long shadow over American law. In law school we had studied their strategies and admired their courage, and we were awed by how they confronted the most important issues of their time. Now I was part of that tradition, and I was nervous. My assignment was the death penalty docket. I honestly could not say at first how I felt about the death penalty. Knowing the signature cruelty some killers showed their victims, I was not automatically opposed. I wasn't sure I could be an effective advocate for such unsavory characters. Is this what social justice was about?

Not long after I started, I was given my first case to handle on my own. It arose the way they all did—as an emergency with an imminent execution date. The defendant had been convicted of first-degree murder, had lost all of his appeals, and was within days of electrocution. An attorney in Montgomery had agreed to challenge his sentence and filed a petition in the Alabama trial court. In less than twenty-four hours, the case was heard and rejected by both the trial court and the Alabama supreme court. The only recourse was an appeal to the federal courts, and the lawyer called LDF for help. I gulped.

I prepared the necessary petitions and sent them to my new cocounsel in Montgomery, who filed them the next day. The federal judge ordered an emergency hearing on our motion to stay the execution, but I could not get there in time to appear in court. My cocounsel was uncomfortable handling the matter without me, so the judge agreed to hear the motion by conference call. We all got on the phone.

"Counsel, state yo' names for the recud," said the judge in a deep southern drawl rich with history and tobacco.

"Deval Patrick for the petitioner," I said, my voice cracking.

"All right then, Mr. Patrick, hold on an' let me hear who's representin' the State of Alabama."

When the assistant attorney general of Alabama identified himself, the judge replied warmly, "Hey there, Ed, how you doin'?"

Oh, brother! I thought. I'm in trouble.

The judge opened the hearing by asking me directly, "Now then, Mr. Patrick, don't you just think there are some people who ought to die?"

"Well, Your Honor, we all will someday," I said. "But this proceeding is about whether his trial was fair."

The judge granted the stay. Our client was within hours of the death chamber by then, having had his last meal and his head shaved (which avoids the unpleasant odor of burning hair at electrocution). The judge even allowed us discovery so the defense team could have access to the prosecutor's files. There we found a sworn statement from an eyewitness positively identifying another man as the killer. Either it had been withheld from the court-appointed defense counsel or it had been disclosed and never used by counsel to build a defense. Either way, my client's constitutional rights had been violated. His conviction and sentence were vacated, and he was granted a new trial.

I had so many cases like this one that I was finally persuaded that there are certain things the government just does not do well. Making irreversible decisions about life and death is one of them.

Voting rights cases lacked the grisly tension of a death-row case, but they were still momentous, and in my three years at LDF, no case drew more interest than a notorious voting rights trial in Selma, Alabama. The year was 1985, and President Reagan's Justice Department accused three civil rights leaders of voting fraud. The case centered on the actions of Albert Turner, an iconic figure in the civil rights movement. He had been Dr. Martin Luther King Jr.'s top lieutenant in Alabama in the 1960s and had helped to organize the march from Selma to Montgomery on March 7, 1965. On that fateful day, which became known as "Bloody Sunday," Turner had been on the Edmund Pettus Bridge when Alabama state troopers bludgeoned and teargassed the civil rights marchers trying to make their way to Montgomery.

Three years later, after Dr. King was killed, Turner had also been part of the funeral procession, leading one of the mules that pulled the wagon to the Atlanta gravesite.

Turner had tried to keep his mentor's dream alive by leading a successful voter registration drive in rural Perry County. Maybe too successful. African Americans had become a strong political voting bloc in Perry County and throughout the state's "black belt," effectively controlling seven of the ten predominantly black counties. At issue was the casting of absentee ballots, which whites had long used and now so too were blacks using. Indeed, with so many black sharecroppers unable to get to the polls on Election Day, absentee ballots had become essential to their electoral participation and success.

The more I learned about the case, the more outraged I became. Albert Turner deserved far better. He had a degree from Alabama A&M, but he would hide that fact when reaching out to the community because he didn't want to appear to be placing himself above less educated residents. He just wanted them to participate in their government. Most of them were elderly, some were frail, but all remembered a time in their own adult lifetimes when

they had been persecuted for voting or intimidated for trying. Turner helped them to overcome those memories and
urged them to exercise their constitutional right to vote.

Federal prosecutors charged Turner, his wife, Evelyn,
and a friend, Spencer Hogue Jr., with altering absentee
ballots after they were cast or otherwise unlawfully influ-
encing the votes. If found guilty, Turner and Hogue would
receive maximum prison sentences of 115 years; Evelyn,
35 years. Huge fines would be assessed as well. After Turner
was indicted, the authorities offered to place him on pro-
bation for five years, with no jail time, if he promised to
stop his political activities. Turner rejected the offer. He
understood what was at stake.

He told reporters, "The indictments came because
blacks have gotten too well organized for political empow-
erment in the Black Belt of Alabama. They didn't spend a
million dollars because they think a few old folks' ballots
were changed." Now he was to be tried for voting fraud
in a courtroom whose large windows opened to a view of
the very Edmund Pettus Bridge he had crossed to secure
blacks' right to vote in the first place.

Judge Emmett R. Cox, a Reagan appointee from Cot-
tonwood, Alabama, presided over the case. Though the
voting had occurred in Perry County, just outside Selma,
Judge Cox empaneled a jury in Mobile and bused them
several hours north to the location of the trial—a move,
we felt, intended to put more whites on the jury than
would have resulted from using the local pool of potential

jurors. During the trial, Judge Cox had dinner occasionally with the lead prosecutor, a conservative firebrand named Jefferson Beauregard Sessions. The whole thing felt too cozy.

Lani Guinier was an exceptionally talented voting rights expert on the LDF staff, revered by junior and senior lawyers alike. She and I worked with a team of lawyers in Alabama to represent the defendants. Soon we felt as though we were really defending an entire community of black residents, mostly sharecroppers. In Perry County alone, more than fifty FBI agents sought out fifteen hundred black families, many in remote corners of the countryside; some of them couldn't read or write. The agents' tactics spread fear and intimidation. For many, it recalled the reign of terror they had experienced just twenty years earlier.

Our defense team, by day, prepared motions, did legal research, and filed pleadings; by night, we visited potential witnesses and those individuals whose votes were allegedly tampered with. It was hard, nerve-racking work. We drove around on unlit, unmarked dirt roads, searching for addresses by asking at the rare house where we saw lights. When we found the right home, we had to win the confidence of the occupants, most of whom were afraid to get involved. We were often followed by FBI agents, or so we presumed when we saw their familiar black Crown Victorias, covered in the same red clay dust that covered everything in the hot Perry County summers. They would follow just far enough back so that we couldn't see into the car and would wait with engines idling when we went into someone's home. The next morning, an agent would appear at the house we had visited or show up in the field or shop where the witness worked and ask what we had talked about the night before. It all had its intended chilling effect.

It was tough to get people to open up to us. We were from out of town, unfamiliar in both appearance and dialect. We were lawyers. Most of the people we met did not know whom to trust anymore. The FBI had led them to believe that they themselves had done something wrong by letting Turner and his colleagues help them with their absentee ballots. Any confidence they may once have had about working together to change the political landscape in Perry County had vanished in the wake of the FBI's intimidating tactics.

Spencer Hogue knew that he would have to ask his neighbors to trust us so we could mount his defense. He called a meeting at a church one night, a tiny, one-room wooden structure on stilts, with no insulation but with a woodstove in the corner and plenty of solid wooden pews. Spencer was a tall, dark-skinned man with dark eyes and massive callused hands—working hands. He was not very talkative and not very articulate when he did speak. He was married to a warm, friendly woman who one sensed kept up both ends of the conversation. He was well respected, the way earnest, consistently reliable men always are. He stood alone, at once commanding and humble, in the pale light in front of the altar. But instead of speaking, he closed his eyes and began by singing in a baritone wail; he started confidently, stomping his foot rhythmically on the rough wooden floor boards and clapping his hands. The audience joined in, many singing along with each familiar verse, some waiting for the chorus, all stamping their feet on the floor and clapping their hands in perfect unison. There were no instruments, no hymnals, just the sweet medley of voices singing, feet thumping, hands slapping. You could feel the swelling confidence. The hymn was followed by Spencer's earnest prayer. What had started as a community meeting turned into a prayer meeting. Only when that was over did we turn to the subject of the trial. But their spirituality, as well as their unity, had given them strength.

It changed everything. Word got around. We started to get the information we needed to build our defense.

Once the proceedings got under way, the trial lasted almost three weeks. It was mean and nasty, marked by angry objections, lengthy bench conferences, and heated cross-examinations. Turner's house was burned down in the middle of it—it felt like one last attempt to intimidate a community that was regaining its voice and courage. No one was arrested. It was a sharp reminder of the cost of taking a stand.

Blessedly, there were lighter moments, too, such as when the famed black defense attorney J. R. Chestnut cross-examined a witness who was well into his eighties and whose youngest son was twelve.

"How old did you say you were?" asked Chestnut, a wily grin on his face. The witness confirmed he was in his eighties.

"And how old is your youngest boy?" Chestnut pressed, incredulous. The witness repeated that the boy was twelve. A juror giggled nervously.

Chestnut scratched his chin and replied, "Sir, there're a whole lot of questions I'd like to ask you, but none of 'em have anything to do with this case." The courtroom erupted with laughter, giving us a needed break from the tension.

Each defendant was entitled to a closing argument, and Chestnut gave the one for Albert Turner. Others of us by then had reviewed the evidence in detail and poked holes in the prosecutors' theory of the case. Chestnut talked about the man. He talked about a man who had been educated at Alabama A&M but who had never really left Perry County, about his work with Dr. King and his sacrifice on the Edmund Pettus Bridge, about his commitment to carry on Dr. King's work by organizing the black community of Perry County, about the countless ways he had helped the witnesses who had been subpoenaed by the government to testify during the trial, about the comforts and opportunities he had given up so he could help his neighbors find a better way forward. Before he delivered every carefully constructed piece of this puzzle, he boomed the refrain "Who *is* Albert Turner?" It was a sermon. By the time he finished, the prosecutors' claim that this man could possibly take advantage of, let alone defraud, his own black brothers and sisters seemed absurd. I was in tears.

The jurors had only been out for a day when we were called back in. The courtroom was packed with the defendants' friends and neighbors, the very people who initially had been too afraid to associate themselves with the trial, let alone come to the courthouse. The jurors somberly entered the hot courtroom and took their seats, unwilling to make eye contact with any of the defendants. Then the verdict was announced: not guilty on all counts. The place erupted with cheers and applause. One of the spectators yelled, "Thank you, jury!" Another started to sing a hymn of thanksgiving, and everyone joined in, just like those irrepressible old ladies of Cosmopolitan. Judge Cox tried to restore order but finally threw down his gavel and stormed off in disgust. Lani and I were in tears again. So were many of the spectators who were singing. We went out to the courthouse steps, gave a brief statement to the press, hopped in our rental car, and a made a beeline for the Montgomery airport.

Jefferson Sessions, the prosecutor, was soon nominated to the Federal District Court in Alabama, but the proposal died in the Senate Judiciary Committee in part because of concerns raised about his voter fraud prosecutions. Ten years later, he was elected to the U.S. Senate, where he serves to this day. Judge Cox was elevated to the

Court of Appeals. My guess is that they will never understand what happened in that courtroom. Those poor old black sharecroppers never lost their faith—in God, in the kindness of the people who were trying to help, and most especially in the hope that justice was still possible. Like the Jean-Pierres, they seemed genuinely proud and even overcome to see that the meek could be vindicated. That's certainly why I was crying.

Several years later, at the Department of Justice, I was again inspired by these types of experiences: moments when the yearning for social justice was met with some affirmation against the odds that it was still possible. During my time in the Civil Rights Division, I was back in Alabama and throughout the South in response to a wave of church burnings, and I had a number of those meetings in backwoods churches, where people prayed for strength and comfort before they got down to the earthly business of solving problems together. These were examples of people seeing their stake in their neighbors' dreams and struggles, as well as their own.

I'd like to think that my commitment to social justice remained consistent even when I wasn't in the public sector. When I became a corporate executive, I tried to maintain a personal pledge to do good—to make the ladies of Cosmopolitan proud.

Not long after I left the Justice Department, private attorneys settled a closely watched employment discrimination case at Texaco, one of the largest oil and gas companies in the world and a storied brand for decades. The company sponsored variety shows on television and Saturday afternoon radio broadcasts of the Metropolitan Opera. Its jingle—"You can trust your car to the man who wears the star"—was familiar to most people in America then over forty.

The settlement required the court to appoint a task force to implement the agreement, essentially a complex set of policies and actions that would completely transform the company's employment policies and practices. I was asked to chair the task force and did so for two years. Eventually the CEO asked me to join the company as general counsel. It was a great opportunity to get a different view of the law and of private sector management. Once the company merged with Chevron and Diane and I decided not to relocate to the new headquarters in San Francisco, I moved to Coca-Cola in a similar capacity in the wake of a similar employment discrimination class-action lawsuit. Again, I was asked to implement changes in the employment practices and to oversee the company's global legal affairs.

I was able to travel around the world to try to solve a great variety of problems in many different cultures—and to make some money as well. Social justice was never far from my mission, even in those corporate settings. I know we made the workplace in both companies more fair and transparent. I worked to make Texaco the first major oil company to stop arguing about the science of climate change and to join those in search of solutions. At Coca-Cola, I worked to resolve serious charges of worker mistreatment at a bottling plant in Colombia and to investigate a whistleblower scandal that ensnared a good, mild-mannered man who was trying to do the right thing. I learned that I need not and would not leave my conscience at the door for any job. Most of the people I worked with shared those values.

Politics presents different challenges to faith. In a world where it seems quite appropriate, even imperative, to address issues of social and economic justice, it can still be surprisingly difficult to accomplish. One tough-minded congressman I have come to know and like worries aloud that I am not mean enough for politics, that people feel they can mess with me and my administration without consequences. He said, "I love you, but I wish you were more of an SOB sometimes." I told him that the reason he loves me is because I'm not. He laughed and admitted it was true.

An important distinction needs to be made in politics between allowing your values to guide you and keeping religion and government separate. Liberals are rightly concerned about government-established and government-supported religion, especially in our religiously polyglot society. But their unwillingness to engage on policy at the level of transcendent and timeless values, for fear of sounding too moralistic or religious, yields too much ground to the radical political right, which has come to claim Christianity in particular to advance a deeply un-Christian agenda. Theirs is a faith based on intolerance, a faith without compassion. Hating homosexuals and despising illegal immigrants instead of hating poverty and despising homelessness seems to miss the point of a life of faithfulness. The Gospel of Matthew teaches us:

> For I was hungry and you gave me something to eat, I was thirsty and you gave me something to drink, I was a stranger and you invited me in, I needed clothes and you clothed me, I was sick and you looked after me, I was in prison and you came to visit me.
>
> Then the righteous will answer him, 'Lord, when did we see you hungry and feed you, or thirsty and give you something to drink? When did we see you a stranger and invite you in, or needing clothes and clothe you? When did we see you sick or in prison and go to visit you?'
>
> The King will reply, 'I tell you the truth, whatever you did for one of the least of these brothers of mine, you did for me.'

Hardly ever does the radical right invoke these truths. While they claim to be the political haven for God-fearing Americans, love—so central to Christianity—has no place in their agenda. When they speak of faith, it seems obscene.

During my campaign for governor in 2006, the question of marriage equality was hotly debated. The Massachusetts Supreme Judicial Court had struck down practices that limited marriage to the union of a man and a woman, and many tried to organize a ballot initiative to overturn the Court's ruling. I agreed with the ruling and supported marriage equality. Churches were deeply divided.

The black church was particularly agitated, in part because the radical right promised that unless the court's decision was overturned, churches would be forced to marry gay and lesbian couples or risk losing their tax-exempt status. My sister and her husband, Bernie, were active in one of the largest black churches in Boston, which was led by a gifted preacher and a leader among the black clergy. He denounced me and my candidacy from the pulpit on many Sundays while Rhonda and Bernie sat in the front pew.

I met with the Black Ministerial Alliance in Boston during the campaign, asking for their support while acknowledging our differences on this issue. I said I believed in a politics that did not require that we agree on everything before we could work together on anything. And I challenged them to work with me on the issues I believed their parishioners cared most about, such as being able to pay their rent and their heating bill in the same month. I'm happy that I got their support in the end, but a lot of nasty things were said. For some of these black ministers, the notion of social justice, faith in action, was secondary.

Once I won and took office, I worked hard to get the necessary votes at the constitutional convention that was convened so that the joint legislature could resolve the question. We convinced enough legislators to support marriage equality and to keep discrimination out of the Massachusetts Constitution. It seemed what faith in action demanded. I had no idea until many months later that our own daughter, Katherine, who was nineteen at the time, was getting ready to come out.

In politics, there are a handful of people whose wealth, connections, and influence are enough to assure that their views will always be taken into account. They have access to those in the White House, the Capitol, and the statehouses across America, regardless of which party is in power. Their calls will be returned, and as governor, I have returned their calls. But if social justice means anything in politics, it means opening up the process to those who have been left out, to hear *their* voices and return *their* calls. I ran for governor in part because I saw that so many people had dropped out of the process and had lost faith in their democracy. Sometimes the press calls them the "have-nots," but I think they have plenty. They just have to be reminded that they have plenty to contribute—they have all the power they need to make the changes they want.

During my first primary campaign, I made a campaign

stop at the Local 26 Union Hall in Boston. Local 26 represents about five thousand workers in the hospitality industries in Greater Boston, and all the candidates were invited to one of their rallies. These were the working poor. For many of them, English was not their first language. The room was crowded and hot. They listened intently, but many shifted and murmured to one another. It was by no means clear they were getting my points.

Midway through my speech I stopped, put away my notes, and just looked at them.

"I want to say something else to you," I said. "I want you to know, I see you."

The room got quiet.

"I know you work places where people look right past you. They walk right past you. I know that. You take their dirty sheets off. You take away their wet towels. And they pass you in the room, they pass you in halls, and they don't make eye contact. They pass you as you're holding the door. They're on their cell phone. They're doing their thing, and they don't see you. Well, I want you to know something."

I paused, took in the entire crowd, and spoke slowly.

"I . . . see . . . you. And I appreciate you."

It was suddenly a completely different room, and I could feel it.

"The reason I want you to come and vote is that I want your government to see you. And that's not going to happen unless you claim a stake in that government. And let me tell you something else. I want you to come and vote for me. But if you don't come and vote for me, that's okay. I understand. But you have to show up, because this is your claim. So stop leaving it to the pundits and the pollsters to tell us whose turn it is, who's supposed to be next, and who's going to win. It's your turn."

The place erupted. I don't think I've ever felt a stronger connection with any group as I did with that one.

As it happens, I was back in that same union hall three years later. The circumstances were quite different.

In August 2009, two Hyatt hotels in Boston and one in Cambridge laid off ninety-eight housekeepers. The workers were mostly black and Hispanic women. Some had been cleaning rooms at Hyatts for more than twenty years. They earned about $15 an hour. The severe recession, of course, caused massive job cuts in Massachusetts and around the country, including ones I had to make in state government, but these layoffs were different. The Hyatt hotels didn't actually reduce staff; they simply replaced the existing housekeepers with lower-paid workers from an employment agency. At my meeting with the housekeepers at the union hall, some of the women had tears in their eyes. They didn't know how they were going to pay for food, rent, and utilities. I was recovering from hip surgery and was using a cane—hardly an inspiring sight—but I held the hands of the women who were now sharing their grief. They told me that Hyatt had asked them to train the new staff members so they could fill in during vacations and holidays. They had no idea they were training their own replacements—who would be making $8 an hour.

There is a mindset in our country among hard right-wingers and free-market purists that poverty is exclusively the fault of the impoverished. They're lazy. They're not motivated. Capitalism produces the greatest good for the greatest number, and if there's collateral damage in the process, so be it.

All that this market fundamentalism is about is letting people's consciences off the hook. If the market is "just," none of us is responsible for the havoc it may wreak. But the invisible hand of the market need not be free of ethical values, and ought not be. In any event, there is a right way to lay off people and a wrong way, and this was the wrong way. The Bible admonishes believers to do justly, to love mercy, and to walk humbly. Secular equivalents in every culture and community require us to respect the dignity of others.

I intervened in the Hyatt dispute to remind this company as well as others that the financial bottom line is not the only bottom line. There is also a community bottom line, an environmental bottom line, a moral bottom line, and public leadership should try to integrate all of them.

I communicated these messages to Hyatt's chief executive in several telephone calls and letters. In one I wrote, "I understand first hand how difficult it is to manage through the current economic challenges without compounding the disruptions the times have caused. But surely there is some way to retain the jobs for your housekeeping staffs, as other hotels have done, and to work with them to help the company meet its current challenges, rather than tossing them out unceremoniously to fend for themselves while the people they trained take their jobs at barely livable wages."

I also warned that I would direct state employees to boycott all Hyatt properties when conducting state business unless the ninety-eight housekeepers were rehired. The threat was more symbolic than anything else. The Commonwealth of Massachusetts does not do enough business with Hyatt hotels to make a dent in their revenues, but I was not alone among public officials in condemning the company. Boston's mayor, Thomas Menino, and U.S. Congressman Michael Capuano, among others, also expressed their outrage. Several hundred hotel workers and their supporters held a loud rally in front of the Hyatt Regency Boston and received ample television coverage. Protests were staged at Hyatts in Chicago and San Francisco. The Boston Taxi Drivers Association vowed to boycott the Hyatt properties unless the housekeepers were given their jobs back. A group of more than two hundred rabbis and cantors from around the country signed a petition saying that Hyatt had not only insulted its workers but insulted the Torah as well.

In the face of this public relations disaster, Hyatt did make some concessions. It offered positions to the housekeepers with the staffing organization that it uses for contract labor. Hyatt said those who accepted the positions would be paid their full Hyatt wages through the end of 2010. Those who didn't accept could opt for a "job preparedness and placement assistance program." Each housekeeper also received an extension of Hyatt health care benefits.

But a mere half dozen of the housekeepers accepted the offer to work at the staffing agency. I wasn't surprised. Those women were not so different from the ladies in the big hats of Cosmopolitan Community Church—compassionate and loving, yes, but also proud and resilient. Once you insult them, you can't expect them to want to be in business with you, let alone scrub your bathrooms.

Whether it's at my church, in my work, or in my daily life, I try not to wear my faith on my sleeve (the ladies of Cosmopolitan would show little patience for that) but to contribute where I can to the common good. It's a struggle. I have a mean temper, my patience can wear thin, and I can be short with people who are short with me. I am definitely still working on "turning the other cheek." But more often than not, I have learned that kindness to friend and foe alike moves me further forward and gives me more lasting satisfaction than any other way of being in the world. As Jesse Jackson once said in an elegant public apology, "God is not finished with me yet."

I also believe that religious faith and social justice

are inextricably linked. If faith is expressed in what you do and how you do it, not in what you claim to believe, then surely we must acknowledge the needs and support the dreams of those around us, those of the meek not just the mighty, and act accordingly.

We Christians believe that Christ will return one day. I've thought about what form Christ will take when he does. I'm pretty sure he will not descend in flowing robes or amid spectral choruses. I think there's a good chance he will be the guy in rags, in an out-of-the-way place somewhere, begging, wondering if anyone sees him.

Chapter 7

OVERCOMING KRYPTONITE

I stink at standardized tests. I never had any real instruction in test-taking skills in the Chicago public schools, and even at Milton my exposure to standardized tests came only through the SATs. I got good scores, but far from the coveted "double 800s." So when it came time for me to take the bar exam after law school, I was apprehensive.

To prepare, I took a bar exam prep course, at great expense, but found the mnemonic devices and instruction at calculated guessing gimmicky. I had been a strong law student, making minor (albeit worthless) history by simultaneously leading the Legal Aid Bureau and winning the Ames moot court competition. I was a successful summer associate at three different, sought-after law firms and had offers to join each one after my clerkship. I was about to start clerking for a renowned federal appellate judge. I knew how to practice, I thought, at a high level. I just needed my license. Surely I could pass a silly old bar exam.

When I learned that I failed in the fall of 1982, I was embarrassed and devastated. I thought it would reflect poorly on the judge and make him and my fellow clerks question whether I was worthy of the job. Fortunately, everyone was encouraging. "The California Bar is the hardest in the country to pass," they said. True, but it was small comfort. I worked doubly hard in the chambers to prove my value and vowed to redeem myself the next time.

I was deep into my clerkship when I took the exam again. I prepared extensively. I was truly invested. It was a matter of pride. I would not fall short.

But I failed again, and the result was a seismic shock, with self-doubt now creeping into my mind. What if I'm not up to this? What if I'd overestimated my abilities all along? Who wouldn't think that? This time, the judge and my fellow clerks just acknowledged the outcome and kept their thoughts to themselves. I thought they were looking at me as they would someone with a deadly disease: with pity, as if they knew I was not long for their world. My sister, one of the few people in whom I confided, worried aloud right with me. "Are you going to be able to practice law?" she asked. I honestly didn't know. In some respects, it was the first time I had ever suffered rejection in an academic setting. Diane was unfailingly confident, which I appreciated, but I had learned that she could fake confidence pretty well if she wanted to.

There was nothing else to do but to try again—to prepare with greater urgency, to forgo Happy Hours and date nights, to invest even more time to meet the challenge. But my confidence remained badly shaken, and in the summer of 1983, when I walked into the convention center in Los Angeles with a couple of thousand other applicants for three full days of examination, I thought I might end up being a banker.

This time I passed, and the feeling was more relief than elation. I take comfort, to be sure, that my struggles with the bar exam were not a precursor to my legal career, which has had many highlights. But to get through my "California crucible" took the kind of concentration and resolve that I had not summoned since my time in Sudan. It was an act of will to quiet the doubt, to restore my faith in myself, and to get the work done.

I have experienced plenty of rejection, like everyone else. Not being picked for either side's stickball team until the very end. Girls I admired and flirted with who would not give me the time of day. Jobs. Bank loans. Important motions in court I thought I should have won. Fancy people I wanted to get to know who ignored me, on more than one occasion by literally and conspicuously turning their backs. Diane and I were encouraged to apply for membership in the Country Club, a venerable retreat in Brookline, Massachusetts, famous for its flawless golf course and its legacy of Brahmin members. I had visited a few times as a guest. But after garnering more "seconders," or endorsements, than any applicant in the history of the club, we learned we were blackballed.

Most rejections were harmless. Some were more pernicious, like the apartments I tried to rent in west Los Angeles: They were available when I called, suddenly weren't when I arrived to look at them, and then miraculously became available again when I called later. One night I had a meeting in the Oval Office with President Clinton. It ran late, and I could not get a cab to stop in front of the White House on Pennsylvania Avenue. Taxis would glide right past me to the white guy down the block.

Growing up as I did, maneuvering through Milton and Harvard, and traveling as I had, I received many lessons about overcoming adversity, large and small. But nothing is as humbling or as insidious as political life.

When I first ran for governor, I certainly knew that I would be subjected to far more criticism than ever before, and if I won, the second-guessing, the carping, and even the personal attacks would become my daily fare. All of that did indeed happen. For the first time, I had not only my judgment assailed but my character impugned. Legitimate complaints should be heeded—no politician or political party has all the answers—but I tried to ignore the crackling static of personal invective and the belittling impulse of our political culture. The same singular focus and concentration I had already learned was needed, I thought, to move our policy agenda forward.

In retrospect, I realize that my approach was a little too narrow. I did not fully consider the larger implications of a public life for my family and did not foresee how the glaring limelight would affect the woman at the center of my life—until it was far too late, until after the blows had been delivered and the wound lay bare and bleeding.

In January of 2005, I had just left my job at Coca-Cola in Atlanta in part because I was tired of the weekly commute from Boston. I'm sure Diane was hoping that my next job would be a little more . . . settled. She was entitled to a husband who was home more often than gone. In addition to running the house and participating in numerous charities, Diane continued her impressive legal career. Since the mid-1990s, she has been with Ropes & Gray in Boston, where she is a valued partner specializing in labor law.

I was eager to live and work closer to home again in Boston, but I was ready to take my career in a different direction. I told Diane that I wanted to run for governor, which stunned her. She asked if I wouldn't consider running for Congress or another office that was a little less ambitious for a first run. But I said that I wanted to set the agenda, and I thought the governor's role was the right one for the contributions I thought I could make. She presumed, like everyone else, that I had little chance of winning, but she knew my track record of accomplishing what I set my mind to.

As always, she supported my decision, but reluctantly this time. We knew that a campaign would put us both in the spotlight, which would be taxing for someone as private as Diane. We knew political campaigns could get nasty, particularly when you throw race into the mix, but we thought we were ready.

In some ways, Diane was more ready than I: For all of her reticence, she was a frighteningly good campaigner—smart, articulate, a model of grace and charm. When we appeared jointly on the campaign trail, I would often hear, "Why isn't *she* running?" And in truth, Diane was excited by the enthusiasm of the crowds, the hoopla and stagecraft of the modern campaign, and thoroughly gratified by the favorable response. But those events are the sheen of any campaign. Beneath the camera lights and confetti are the efforts to smear and undermine candidates, and they rise to the surface quickly.

Early in the primary race, there were attempts to embarrass us about a house we were building in western Massachusetts on land we had owned for many years. Aerial photographs of the construction appeared in the newspapers with exaggerated claims about the scope of the project and false charges that we had clear-cut a large swath of forested mountainside. One candidate called the house the "Taj Deval." It was as if I had made some breach with the public—as if Ted Kennedy or Mitt Romney or John Kerry could own a nice home, but not Deval Patrick. I considered what the fuss said about the state of politics and the character of my opponents, and said so. Diane found herself suddenly embarrassed about a project we had dreamt about and worked toward for decades.

That controversy passed, but others followed. My Republican opponent wanted to portray me as "soft on crime" because, while at the Legal Defense Fund, I had helped a man convicted of murdering a policeman appeal his death sentence. She ran an attack ad that asked, "While lawyers have a right to defend admitted cop-killers, do we really want one as our governor?" (I assume she meant, do we want "such a lawyer as our governor," not a cop-killer.) In another matter, I had urged Massachusetts to conduct a DNA test on a convicted rapist whose guilt seemed in doubt. So another attack ad cast me as a friend of sexual predators and played into racist fears about black men and white women: The camera followed a woman walking through a dark garage, then viewers heard an interview with me in which I described the prisoner, with whom I had exchanged letters, as "thoughtful." The voiceover said, "Have you ever heard a woman compliment a rapist?" (For the record, the DNA test confirmed the man's guilt.) I had a campaign staff and a cadre of energetic volunteers to help me with this nonsense, but it took its toll.

The most egregious ploy occurred three weeks before the general election, when the *Boston Herald* published a story about my brother-in-law; thirteen years earlier, he had pleaded guilty to sexually assaulting my sister. After serving a short jail sentence, the two reconciled and moved to Massachusetts with their children to be near us. They became deacons in their church, live a deeply religious life, work hard, bought and refurbished a home, and raised two wonderful children who are a constant presence in our lives. The article said that my brother-in-law had unlawfully failed to register with the state's Sex Offender Registry Board, a fact that could have been published only if the Board had unlawfully disclosed that information to the newspaper. The claim was wrong regardless; as a court later confirmed, he did not have to register. But the article embarrassed my sister and brother-in-law publicly, exposed their children to information they had not known, and cost my brother-in-law his job and his family's health benefits. For a time, it ruined their lives. As *USA Today* wrote about the episode, "How sick is this?"

I was often asked how I felt about these and other sordid political tactics and what impact they had on me. But I was never asked what impact they had on my wife. Political spouses are often forgotten. I worried about these ads politically, but Diane absorbed them personally. I knew the campaign was exacting a toll on her, but I did not appreciate how deeply. She was angry that my character had been called into question, that our privacy had been invaded unnecessarily, and that good people we loved had been damaged.

We were all under a lot of stress, and I assumed that this was typical in a campaign. But Diane's frustrations came to a boil when she was on a business trip in California and she received word that the *Boston Globe* was going to publish a story alleging that years before we had defaulted on a mortgage. Diane wanted no part of this controversy, but in our household she keeps the financial records, so she was inevitably drawn into the defense.

The story itself was false. To our amazement, the *Globe* wouldn't tell us why it thought we had defaulted or what proof it had, but we found ourselves having to prove the story was false to prevent it from running. The campaign was concerned. How do you prove something didn't happen? It fell to Diane to do just that. She flew back home in a panic and sat down in the long back hall outside the dark closet where we kept old file cabinets and systematically unpacked box after box of canceled checks and dusty old statements. (Thankfully, she's a pack rat). She eventually found the canceled check for the final payment as well as the final statement. She handed them over to the campaign, which gave them to the *Globe*. The story was killed.

But the episode pushed Diane to her limit. She told me then that the stress was getting to her, that she couldn't be on call twenty-four hours a day to put out fires, that she had a job and a career that she couldn't and wouldn't sacrifice for my political ambitions. She couldn't sleep and was tired and despondent. I promised I would try to protect her from the media queries, but I couldn't protect her from the rumors. One alleged that I had used cocaine. How did that get started? Someone had heard that I was "involved with Coke," referring to my time at Coca-Cola, and it took off from there. Even suggestions that were meant to be helpful were absurdly personal. At a public event in the Berkshires, Diane was approached by a woman who said she needed better "foundations"—not spiritual or moral, but undergarments. Diane was taken aback, and she later shared this story with a few others at a fundraiser in Boston. A woman she didn't know soon approached her and said, "I hear you're in the market for foundations. Well, I have a great guy." The woman then unbuttoned her blouse. "Look how large I am," she said. "You could use a good foundation too."

Any politician will tell you that the hothouse of a close campaign can obliterate the fine line between your public and private lives. When you run for office, that's what you sign up for. But in Diane's case, I didn't realize that that feeling—that sense of losing control of your own life, of the world closing in on you, of suffocating—was both familiar and haunting. It had happened in her first marriage, when Bill succeeded in redefining who she was. Now, it was the media and our political opponents who were redefining who I was and, indirectly, who she was. Diane has a clear image of herself as a mother, a lawyer, a volunteer, and a community activist, but now she was being cast solely as "Deval Patrick's lovely wife, Diane," or misidentified as my "lovely wife, Donna." (Another time, she was "Shirley.")

Even though Diane remained ambivalent about the campaign, she continued to campaign brilliantly—sometimes with me, sometimes on her own. Perhaps the very openness that had made her vulnerable to Bill's abuse also allowed her to connect so well to others. She listens well and is genuinely empathic. People would draw her aside and say that they could tell I was a good man because she was "so real." The reaction in African-American audiences was also relief. More than a few people whispered to her, "Honey, I'm so glad to see you are black!" So many educated and accomplished African-American men marry across racial lines that it was presumed I had, too. Perhaps because I was a newcomer to the political scene, perhaps because I was the first black Democratic nominee, perhaps because we were running a kind of insurgent campaign, I think voters needed to feel comfortable with me as their prospective governor, and Diane came to play an outsized role in the campaign. Quite honestly, I don't know that I would have won without her.

The morning after the election, Diane awoke in a state of disbelief. Was this really happening? She was exhausted, and I can't deny that she deserved better from me. I had turned fifty that year, and Diane had thrown a wonderful party for me in July. She also planned a family trip to South Africa over Christmas (a major undertaking that was shortened because of our victory). Diane's birthday came in December, in the midst of the transition and shortly before we were to leave for South Africa. It was on a Sunday. I envisioned a quiet day with the family and did not make any other plans. On our way home from services at Memorial Church in Harvard Yard, I asked Diane what she wanted to do. It was the wrong question. Given all of her sacrifices over the previous two years, she was sure I had organized something to make this day extra special. She started to cry. My apologies fell on deaf ears and damp cheeks.

I tried to convince myself that things would improve once we moved into our jobs as governor and first lady, when we could focus on getting things done rather than the hype of the campaign. But we were at the center of high political drama: a black man had just come from nowhere to win a decisive victory with a promise to change Beacon Hill, and the pundits and pollsters appreciated even better than I how formidable a task lay ahead of me. The fish bowl would only get smaller, the pressures greater. The same "wise guys" who had said I couldn't win were now saying I couldn't govern.

Several weeks after the election, Diane and I went to a seminar at the Greenbrier Resort in West Virginia for new governors from across the country. We were to learn how to make the transition from running a campaign to running a state. The "first spouses" were also there for guidance. For Diane, it was all very strange. She attended seminars on how to dress for television (avoid stripes and polka dots) and how to conduct yourself in interviews (stick to the script). Mock interviews were filmed and analyzed. There were sessions on how the first spouse should raise money for the state mansion and how to manage a household staff. Well, Massachusetts has no governor's residence, and Diane had no plans to assemble a staff of any kind.

Other spouses told Diane that her new responsibilities would force her to leave her job, but she explained that she thoroughly enjoyed her job. "Believe me, honey," someone said, "within a year you won't be working anymore." At the very least, Diane was informed, she would need to hire a chief of staff to help with everything from scheduling to fielding the daily barrage of requests and inquiries that would now be part of her life to sending out Christmas cards.

Already shaky from the campaign, Diane had even more reason to feel overwhelmed. Several weeks later, she took the advice she had received from experienced spouses and hired a chief of staff. Amy Gorin, an old and trusted friend who had been the cochair of my campaign, had already traveled extensively with Diane and knew her well. Diane trusted her. The move seemed unexceptional—if the first lady of Guam had a chief of staff, why wouldn't the first lady of Massachusetts?

If only it had been that simple. The next thing we

knew, Diane was getting pummeled by the press. She was cast as a spoiled brat, a high-paid lawyer who felt so entitled that she could use state money to get someone to write her letters. She felt she had no way to defend herself. That controversy came on the heels of the media's scolding me for trying to furnish the office properly (when I arrived, the furniture consisted of a desk whose handles came off when you pulled them and a table with a broken leg; hardly suitable for projecting a positive image of the state, I thought) and for leasing a Cadillac (the same car nearly every governor east of the Mississippi drove; the *Herald*'s description of the car as "tricked-out" struck some people, including Diane, as racist).

I paid for the office furnishings and the car out of my own pocket. Diane let her chief of staff go and assumed all the responsibilities of first lady on her own. Grudgingly, the items left the news, but not before the media had a field day—"Coupe Deval" and "Together We Con." It made me feel silly and even a little bitter at first. The worst was the condescension of the political hacks, who were reluctant to take me seriously on a good day and who treated my early gaffes as a reason not to deal with our substantive agenda.

Learning eventually to keep my guard up in political life, I rarely answered directly when asked if there were things about those early weeks I regretted. Of course I felt disappointed, angry, and even bitter, mainly at myself. But I had learned to channel those emotions into something positive. That's how I had put setbacks behind me in the past—by climbing the next mountain. So I set about trying to pursue the very goals that had motivated me to become governor in the first place. Even after I delivered on many of the big initiatives we had promised in the campaign and successfully steered state government through the worst economic downturn since the Great Depression, the media could not resist recalling those early missteps. But I kept going, kept producing, remembering that at the end of the day, history will judge me not by the symbols of office but by the substance of our accomplishments and their impact on the lives of people.

Unfortunately, it was not so straightforward for Diane. For as long as I've known her, she has read the newspaper each morning before doing anything else. She craved the information to feel connected to the community and to the culture at large. The newspaper itself seemed to bring clarity and order to her world. It was once a healthy addiction, but now it was torture.

"Reading the paper," she told me one day, "makes me nervous and weak. It feels like kryptonite."

"Then stop reading the newspaper," I said. "Do you think Superman seeks out kryptonite?" I thought it was that simple.

I had been consumed with the campaign and then with the immediate demands of my new job. I knew that expectations were high, that I would be held to a different standard, and I was eager to serve with class, thoughtfulness, and professionalism, so I was busy poring over résumés to find outstanding appointees for the cabinet and trying to understand the intricacies of the state budget. I was conscientious about serving the people of Massachusetts, but I did not serve the most important person in my life. I didn't realize how badly Diane was hurting. When our official photograph was taken as governor and first lady of Massachusetts, she wore a radiant red jacket but could barely muster a smile. She felt that she had lost control over her life and was spiraling into depression.

One night in early March of 2007, about nine weeks into my new job, I told Diane about an article that would appear the next day. The *Globe* would report about a call I had made to Citibank. I spoke as a character reference for the executives of a company on whose board I had once sat. It was innocent but dumb, and the insinuations were about to fly. Was I using my position as governor rather than my prior personal relationships to influence the bank? Did I stand to gain financially? Had I violated the state ethics rules? (I had not.) We turned off the lights, but Diane awoke after a fitful sleep. She nudged me awake and said she just couldn't face another critical story. She began to cry and shake. When I asked her what was wrong, she said, "I just hate this. I hate this. This is what the next four years are going to be like."

Her heart was racing, and her skin was cold and clammy. (Our daughters were away at school, so just the two of us were at home.) At first, I thought she was having a heart attack. I couldn't console her. She was in a panic and unraveling.

"I don't want to get up," she said. "I can't do this anymore."

Years earlier, she had seen a therapist in Boston, so I called her, and she suggested that I take Diane to the hospital. "Let's admit her medically," she said. She thought McLean Hospital, a psychiatric facility, was the right place for her, and she would meet us there. Diane wasn't suicidal, but she needed to be away from this reality. I then spoke to Diane. "I want you to do this," I said. "How do you feel about it?"

"Yes," she said. "I just don't feel right."

A state trooper drove us to McLean, and on the 45-minute drive over, Diane held my hand and kept repeating, "I'm so sorry, I'm so sorry."

"Please stop," I told her. I was the one who was sorry.

McLean has a private entrance, but we still had to wait in a parking lot until the coast was clear. Once she was taken to an admissions room, I was asked to sit in the stairwell, out of sight, during the intake interview. She was finally admitted under a false name, "Jennifer Blake." It was scary for her, surreal for me.

For the next several days, Diane rested and worked with her therapist, a truly caring and able woman who was our strongest advocate throughout Diane's recovery. Her sister, Lynn, came up from Atlanta and spent time with her while I was at work. Diane took a battery of tests: IQ tests, physical tests, stress tests. We then met to discuss the results. The doctors concluded that she was extremely smart but was obsessed with always doing the right thing perfectly, being perceived in the right light—and felt she would pay a huge price if she wasn't. They helped her see that she had the strength and intelligence to overcome those insecurities, but she needed to understand her own limits. Medication was prescribed to help her rest, and with the help of her sister, her therapist, and others, she began to drill down to her own emotional core.

Her anger at the media had not dissipated, and she felt that she and I had been treated unfairly. While in the hospital, she read the National Governors Association website to learn what type of support other first ladies had. Some had drivers on their staffs; others had flower arrangers. The first lady of California had a $500,000 budget, two correspondence secretaries, a chief of staff, a driver, and a robust website. Diane had no staff, no budget, no state residence, nothing—but she had been humiliated for hiring one person to help her do the unpaid job of first lady. She wrote a sizzling letter to the *Globe* that conveyed her feelings of betrayal. She asked both me and her therapist to read it first, and we advised her not to send it. At this point, creating even more tension with the media was not going to improve her health. I told the McLean staff to stop delivering the *Globe* to Diane's room. The kryptonite wasn't helping.

Over dinner one night at the hospital, we got to talking about the public life we were living. "You were proud that I won," I said. "But you were hoping I'd lose."

She looked at me in stunned silence for a long time. "How did you know that?" It was true.

For the first several days at McLean, we placed a premium on secrecy. The doctors felt that the stigma of mental illness and the meanness of the media would not be useful. For the first few days, even my staff did not know; I literally sneaked in and out of the hospital in the evenings. (One thing I have noticed about being a black man: If you're dressed in jeans and a casual shirt with a cap on, people will often look right past you.)

But Diane was worried that the story would leak, and we would be chasing it instead of being forthright. She was also tired of being ashamed, of feeling bad.

"I don't like you sneaking in and out of here to see me," she said. "I'm not ashamed of not feeling well. I think we should tell people I'm here so we get ahead of it."

She knew it was going to hurt—talking about mental illness is the ultimate sacrifice of privacy—but she felt that was the better option. I supported her, but the doctors thought it was a big mistake. "Diane's already dealing with profound stress because of public scrutiny," the chief resident told us. "This will make it much worse."

Diane knew, however, that at some point, she was going to have to face her friends, her colleagues, and her clients, and she wanted them to know the truth. It was also the reassertion of her control over her own circumstances, and it struck me as amazingly brave. Besides, her medical team, her sister, and I were right there to help her deal with the reaction.

My office released a brief statement: "First Lady Diane Patrick is being treated for exhaustion and depression. The governor will work a flexible schedule for the next few weeks in order to spend more time with her and his family. The family asks for the prayers and understanding of the public."

Then we waited.

We had long conversations about the possibility of my resigning and resuming our private lives. There were moments when I was willing—being governor is an episode in my life; Diane *is* my life—but she didn't want to feel responsible for giving up something we had worked so hard for. There were other moments when Diane, imagining the resumption of her role as first lady, asked me to quit, but I said we should wait to decide until she got out of the hospital.

Ultimately, we decided together that I would continue as governor, and it was for the best. If I had resigned, it would have appeared as if the pressures had forced Diane into the hospital and me out of office. The reality was that Diane's difficulties were far more complex and could be traced to her first marriage and even to her childhood. And given how hard so many people had worked for us—how much hope people had invested in us during the campaign—I wanted to complete my term and carry through on my promises.

What was most gratifying was the response Diane received to the announcement. The letters and cards began coming in, many from others who had suffered from mental illness, often hiding it for years. Colleagues, friends, legislators and others in public life, their spouses, total strangers—they thanked her for going public. Schoolchildren sent letters, poems, and pictures. One woman knitted a prayer shawl. E-mails came from overseas. Even the media displayed a restraint and respectfulness that was reassuring, even touching. I would carry boxes of letters to the hospital. Thousands would eventually write.

Some letters said we care about you.

Many said we're praying for you.

Others: we love you.

Diane drew strength from this outpouring of affection and support, and she believed she had to be strong for those individuals. Each one made her "incrementally brave," she likes to say. She was released from the hospital after two weeks and was soon ready to return to her job. Her first day back, she woke up, put on her suit, and told me, "I'm back." She resumed devouring the morning newspaper.

Since then, she has given many public speeches about her experiences. After one such appearance, a woman told Diane that she was alive today because Diane's openness made her think that "if the first lady can publicly acknowledge her illness—and survive—then surely I can acknowledge mine to myself and get help." Television reporters have interviewed her, mental health organizations have given her awards, and she continues skillfully to juggle her full-time responsibilities as lawyer, mother, wife, community activist, and first lady of Massachusetts.

In many ways, the political adversity I've faced as governor has paled in comparison to the personal adversity Diane has faced, so it's entirely fitting that her poll numbers, if tracked, would be higher than mine. Hers is the lesson that endures. It would have been easy for this intensely private woman to quit her public life and just lie low until my term in office ended. But she took the hard road traveled by heroines. She did not give in but fought to overcome her circumstances. She did not try to go it alone but sought help from friends, family, and professionals. She did not engage in self-pity but took responsibility for her own well-being. She was not too proud to acknowledge her own limitations.

By speaking out, she has helped remove the stigma of mental illness and—I believe—given courage to anyone who has a disease to be open about his or her condition, to seek help when necessary, and to strive to be a role model for others. She is amazed at her own strength. The people of the Commonwealth—and the governor—are awed by it.

Chapter 8

I was six or seven years old the first time I heard Dr. Martin Luther King Jr. speak. He was addressing a crowd in a park on the South Side of Chicago, and my mother took my sister and me to see him. The crowd seemed large to my child's eyes and solemn, like church. I remember none of King's words from that afternoon, but I remember the sense of optimism. Long before I knew the clarity of King's vision or the power of his imagery, I understood that hope is a tangible thing. I could feel it.

Even at that early age, I had already sensed that I did

not belong in some parts of town and that there were paths through life that were not for me. I knew that I was not liked by people I had never even met. Yet with such moral certainty and command, King made me feel not only that I was welcome at the table but that the feast was as much mine as anyone else's. He was the consummate idealist who made us believe that we could perfect our community and our country.

Idealism is vital. It sustains the human soul. The ability to imagine a better place, a better way of doing things, a better way of being in the world is far more than wishful thinking. It is the essential ingredient in human progress.

Idealism built America. The persecuted religious refugees who set out over a vast ocean in small wooden boats with barely a notion of what awaited them in the New World were fortified mainly by an ideal of the community they wished to create. Just before some of the newest settlers arrived in New England in 1630, John Winthrop, the first governor of Massachusetts, gave an oft-quoted sermon aboard the *Arbella* in which he acknowledged the grand experiment they were about to launch. "For we must consider that we shall be as a city upon a hill," he said. "The eyes of all people are upon us." They imagined a new kind of community, and they reached for it.

That idealism has always been at the core of our national character. From building a new society in a wilderness to ending slavery, from the Industrial Revolution to land grant colleges, from social security to the civil rights revolution to, more recently, national health care reform, Americans have envisioned bold improvements and created new realities. Ours may be the only nation in human history not organized around a common language or religion or culture so much as a common set of civic ideals. And we have defined those ideals over time and through struggle as equality, opportunity, and fair play. For centuries, our perennial challenge has been the gap between our reality and our ideals. Our great strength is that we repeatedly confront that challenge. We keep asking ourselves how our actions measure up. When we are true to our ideals, we are at our best and are justifiably proud. And we are an inspiration to the world.

Idealism is magnetic for me. It explains so many of not only our national triumphs, but my personal ones as well. As a father, husband, and friend, I have tried to demonstrate that idealism can be a lodestar to guide your life. As a lawyer, civil rights advocate, and political leader, I have tried to inspire hope. I value the leaders who have come to see our highest calling as giving someone else a reason to believe.

Even when so many of our national achievements have been the product of this faith in the unseen, we discredit visionaries. For every Lincoln, FDR, or Kennedy, dozens of other political and public leaders were ready to replace a beacon of hope with the flag of surrender. Unfortunately, cynicism is not limited to politicians or the world-weary.

Nowadays, even young people wallow in low expectations. The media and popular culture, reflecting their own limited vision, peddle cynicism like a drug, dulling the senses against hope and celebrating scornful indifference. But the truth is that cynicism is despair in toxic measure. It passes for sophistication. It is mistaken for being "cool." It attempts to be a surrogate for inner strength but fails every time. It is simply a way of giving up on life, the world, and oneself. Good and able people try to make a difference, confront setbacks, and cope with their disappointment by curbing their passion. Cynicism becomes the scab over their wounded idealism. But it doesn't have to be that way.

Mark Twain's childhood dream was to become a riverboat pilot. As a boy in the late nineteenth century, Twain obsessed about learning to navigate a riverboat on the Mississippi River and wanted the prestige and command that went with the job. In *Life on the Mississippi*, he recounts his journey to fulfill his dream. He describes learning to "read" the river like an expert but losing the sense of awe that had drawn him to piloting in the first place. He wrote:

> Now when I had mastered the language of this water and had come to know every trifling feature that bordered the great river as familiarly as I knew the letters of the alphabet, I had made a valuable acquisition. But I had lost something, too. I had lost something which could never be restored to me while I lived. All the grace, the

beauty, the poetry had gone out of the majestic river . . . All the value any feature of it had for me now was the amount of usefulness it could furnish toward compassing the safe piloting of a steamboat. Since those days, I have pitied doctors from my heart. What does the lovely flush in a beauty's cheek mean to a doctor but a "break" that ripples above some deadly disease? Are not all her visible charms sown thick with what are to him the signs and symbols of hidden decay? Does he ever see beauty at all, or doesn't he simply view her professionally, and comment upon her unwholesome condition all to himself? And doesn't he sometimes wonder whether he has gained most or lost most by learning his trade?

And yet, as other passages reveal, even after learning the hazards of the Mississippi that lay beneath her beauty, he is still able to evoke and love her charms, to see her qualities, to feel his own passion about life on the river. His ability to overcome even the most sabotaging moments of cynicism and despair is his triumph.

Everyone, especially young people, must learn that their ideals need not be casualties of their confrontations with reality. I learned this early, from what Dr. King and so many others tried to convey to me, and that lesson itself was a gift. It has made all the difference. I have had my setbacks and outright failures, like anyone else. But I have managed to avoid the apathy, pessimism, and even immobilizing sadness that so often come in the wake of struggle. Idealism is an act of will, to be sure. But we are all up to it—and nothing of any lasting value happens without it.

That lesson must be learned again and again, generation after generation, because I am convinced that cynicism, spawned by disappointment, cultivated by the media, and perpetuated by too many leaders today, holds us back. The courage to look a challenge straight in the eye, to measure our reality against our ideals, and to strive to close the distance between the two has been the hallmark of the American experience. Cynicism is the greatest challenge to that tradition. All of us, but especially young people, must learn to resist it, to nurture our optimism, and to imbue that idealism in others.

That skill comes more naturally to some than others. When I worked for President Clinton in the Justice Department, I remember being struck by his oratorical and political skills. He was a master at reading public opinion. At the same time, he had little appetite for shaping it. Once, not long after I had been appointed, he called me while I was back in Boston for the weekend. I was standing near the checkout counter in the Sears at the South Shore Plaza, not far from our home, when the bulky government cell phone rang.

"Mr. Patrick, this is the White House operator calling," said a brisk, authoritative voice. "Please hold for the president."

"Wait, wait," I said, flustered. "I'm in the middle of a mall. May I find a quiet place and call right back?"

I got a number and made my way to the hair salon where my sister worked, on the second floor of the mall. She let me sit in a supply closet, where I could close the door. I immediately got the president on the line. He was planning to travel to the University of Texas to give a speech, and he wanted me to suggest some text to inspire the students.

"Tell them that you know there are idealists among them, and that you believe in them," I said. I tried to explain the power of having the president of the United States affirm their highest aspirations. I could tell he was skeptical; he did not want to raise anyone's expectations too high. There is probably no more skilled politician in this generation than Bill Clinton, and his presidency, not-withstanding his personal shortcomings, was substantively among the most successful ever. But he was cautious about trying to inspire people.

Barack Obama, on the other hand, understands and embraces his role as an aspirational leader. It's funny how many people presume that, because we are both black politicians with roots in Chicago, we've been friends all our lives. We didn't actually meet until 1995, when I was at the Justice Department. Abner Mikva, then the White

House counsel, was a great progressive in his own right. He had served as a congressman from Chicago and as a federal court of appeals judge in Washington, D.C., and I had gotten to know him during policy debates with the White House staff. Mikva was an adjunct professor at the University of Chicago Law School and knew a young black attorney there who was practicing voting rights law. At lunch in the White House mess one afternoon, he leaned in close.

"Have you met Barack Obama?" he asked.

"The name is familiar," I said.

He encouraged me to meet Obama for a cup of coffee the next time I was in Chicago. When I did, I saw what he and others had found so captivating—Obama's intelligence, idealism, and determination to make a difference in others' lives. Here's a guy to watch, I thought, and over the years, we stayed in touch.

By 2004, I was desperate for aspirational leadership. My frustrations with the Bush presidency had been rising steadily. I felt the Republicans had led us down a dangerous path—a huge debt, an ill-advised war, and the undue curtailing of our personal liberties in the name of national security. I do not accept all of the perceived wisdom of the Democratic Party, and some of the ideas associated with the Republican Party are appealing. Most people aren't buying 100 percent of what either party is selling. But the country needed change. I did not know John Kerry well, but what I knew I liked. He's smart about public policy and has a warmth and wit that do not always come through on television. Throughout his primary campaign, he tapped a yearning for change felt by many Democrats, but something was missing. It was clear that we Democrats were united against Bush and his policies. It became less and less clear, however, what we were *for*.

Then Obama addressed the Democratic National Convention in Boston. I had been at the convention the night before and had tickets for the night that Obama was to deliver the keynote address, but we were at home instead hosting a party for friends who had come from out of town for the convention. Obama was the Democratic candidate from Illinois for the Senate, but he had no national standing. He was little known to most of the political sophisticates at my house as well.

Many politicians pay lip service to hope and idealism, but Obama's appeal in his speech was so clearly heartfelt that it lifted the crowd. After acknowledging the "spin masters" who embrace "the politics of anything goes," he declared:

> We are one people, all of us pledging allegiance to the stars and stripes, all of us defending the United States of America. In the end, that's what this election is about. Do we participate in a politics of cynicism or do we participate in a politics of hope . . . ?
>
> I'm not talking about blind optimism here—the almost willful ignorance that thinks

unemployment will go away if we just don't think about it, or the health care crisis will solve itself if we just ignore it. That's not what I'm talking about. I'm talking about something more substantial.

It's the hope of slaves sitting around a fire singing freedom songs. The hope of immigrants setting out for distant shores. . . .

The hope of a skinny kid with a funny name who believes that America has a place for him, too.

Hope in the face of difficulty. Hope in the face of uncertainty. The audacity of hope!

As soon as Obama finished his speech, one of our guests said, "That will change the calculation for 2008." At last someone had invoked the language of idealism that I was longing for. Because Kerry had personally asked Obama to open the convention, I thought it reflected well on the tone he was trying to set for the party and on the general election campaign.

But his campaign seemed more focused on how to win than on why he should. Kerry was given a perfect opportunity to distinguish himself from Bush in the summer of 2004 when a bipartisan commission issued a damning report on the run-up to the American invasion of Iraq. The weapons of mass destruction, used by Bush to justify his decision to go to war, did not exist. Both candidates were asked: Had you known then what you know now—that there were no weapons of mass destruction—would you have still invaded Iraq?

Bush immediately said yes. Kerry dawdled for three days, and many assumed he was conducting a poll to determine the best answer or the best way to frame it. I furiously shot off e-mails to Kerry's brother, a prominent Boston lawyer who was central to the campaign. I thought Kerry had a chance to present a different vision for using American military force while confronting the Bush administration for its carelessness in starting the war. Instead, he answered the question by agreeing with Bush. I was certain it was not what he believed.

At that moment, the air went out of the campaign for me and many others. I put on a brave face, of course, and helped where I could. But it seemed to me that the Democrats had lost the will to champion values and to be a voice of optimism. At a minimum, that meant rejecting the radical idea of preemptive war when there was no imminent threat to the nation.

I was still working at Coca-Cola at the time, but that's when the seed was planted that I wanted to run for governor. The outcome of the Bush-Kerry contest was close. I was in the campaign suite in the Copley Place Hotel in Boston in the early hours of November 3 when the call was finally made that the race was over. I was thoroughly disappointed, though none could be more than the people around me who had dedicated so much to the campaign,

and I left the suite quickly to avoid the inevitable recrimi-
nations. But I did wonder if the American people had
been allowed to glimpse the real John Kerry or been given
a reason for why his victory mattered to the nation. Here
was an uncommonly decent man, who had sacrificed for
his country and would lead with fortitude and worldliness.
Would our knowing his values and ideals have mattered?
Would knowing mine?

Obama won the Senate seat, of course. Not long after
he was sworn in, I went to Washington to meet with him
in his cramped basement office in the Russell building.
The standard government furniture was still being moved
in. He was himself: long, perilously lanky, relaxed, confident, and a little preoccupied. His eyes are deep and considering; his ears, famously wide. His hands are surprisingly
delicate. We discussed staffing—he had hired an assistant
who had worked for me at Justice—and the oddity of being
a celebrity in an institution that values seniority above all
else. He was looking forward to finding out about his committee assignments.

Then I told him that I was thinking of running for
governor.

"Are you sure?" he asked.

"Yes," I said.

"You got any money?"

"No."

"You got any name recognition?"

"No."

"You got any staff or consultants yet?"

"No."

I said what I did have was a passion for helping people, a willingness to make the tough calls if they are the right ones, and a hunger to reach out to people who were not feeling connected to their government. Above all was my determination to run on my values—win or lose. Democrats, I said, needed to regain their voice of optimism, but a voice that blended optimism with pragmatism, and we needed to put hard questions to our own family members—organized labor, teachers, people of color, public employees, everyone. I didn't know whether I could win, but I thought a little authenticity might count for something in Massachusetts.

I sat on the brown leather sofa of the type and kind that adorns every federal office. Obama sat opposite me on a leather and wooden chair that was also standard issue. He leaned back in his chair and rocked on the two back legs, looking first at me and then into the middle distance. After a few minutes he spoke.

"I'm in," he said. "What do you want me to do?"

Suddenly I had my first major political endorsement. I was grateful. Notwithstanding his skepticism, Obama was exuberant. He immediately proposed to come to Massachusetts for a fundraiser, but I told him it was too early. My own senators weren't on board yet; no point in embarrassing them.

"Oh, yeah," he remembered. "They are my colleagues." We were both new to the big leagues.

Idealism was the theme of my first race for governor. I found I couldn't make a case for changing our policies without also talking about changing our broken politics, about fixing our "broken civic life." Acknowledging how disillusioned so many of our citizens had become, I urged those who had lost faith in their public leaders to return to the political process and to renew their belief that they could make a difference. Against the urging of many of my own supporters and political advisers, we shunned negative ads and maintained a positive message of hope and change.

I was called everything from naive to an "empty suit." Supporters were cautious, as detractors made idealism seem either misleading or dumb. All that led to a remarkable exchange at a candidates' forum in the general election. The moderator asked each of us to say something positive about the other candidate. I complimented the Republican nominee, Kerry Healey, for putting her ideas and her vision on the line and subjecting them to scrutiny and criticism. She had been a leader in response to substance abuse in teenagers as well, and I may have acknowledged that, too. When her turn came, she said rather grudgingly, "Well, he can give a good speech."

Healey's campaign made some withering attacks on my

ideas, my experience, my character, and even my family. It was classic fear-mongering, and I was convinced that people were tired of it. When she dismissed what I was trying to get across in my stump speech, it somehow cut to the core of what I was trying to do in the campaign, to ask people to think and act big, to reach beyond our collective grasp. At a late campaign rally, we hit back, calling out her crucial misunderstanding of what our campaign was all about.

"Healey says that all I can do is give a good speech," I said. "It's just words, she says."

I paused. Then, "'We hold these truths to be self-evident, that all men are created equal.' Just words?"

I was warming up. "'We have nothing to fear but fear itself.' Just words?"

And another one: "'Ask not what your country can do for you. Ask what you can do for your country.' Just words?"

The clincher: "'I have a dream.' Just words?"

Let me be clear: I am no Dr. King, no President Kennedy, no FDR, no Thomas Jefferson. But I do know that certain words survive because they are the indispensable language of inspiration and resolve. No ten-point plan is inscribed on any wall or monument in Washington, D.C. Words that matter capture a noble sentiment, an enduring ideal, a heroic vision. And the right words, spoken from the heart, are a call to action.

The night I was elected governor, I began my acceptance speech by saying that the people of Massachusetts had taken back their government. Then I said, "This was not a victory just for me. This was not a victory just for Democrats. This was a victory for hope."

Hope, it turns out, was springing eternal.

In early 2006, Barack Obama began to toss around the idea of running for president among his friends and staff. Word then got out. He was a junior senator in the third year of his first term and had never run anything larger than a community organization, so he was vulnerable to charges of inexperience. He was aware of his political celebrity but cautious not to make too much of it for fear of seeming presumptuous. He was black. Was the country ready for him?

He announced his candidacy in February 2007. Before a huge, enthusiastic crowd in Springfield, Illinois, he ignited a nervous sense of possibility. Speculation naturally turned to whether he could win; the general consensus was negative. Diane and I had dinner with a fellow governor and her husband one summer evening during a governors' retreat in upstate Michigan. I was new to the job and still tiptoeing around the veteran politicians, trying to avoid political conversations the way one might in any new company. Not Diane. She broke the ice by asking the governor her thoughts about the field of probable candidates, including the favorite Democrat, Hillary Clinton. The governor said flatly that Clinton could not win and that "Barack should." In conversations like that one, repeated over and over among politicians and casual observers alike, I began to sense that what people wanted most was a reason to hope. They wanted to be inspired. They wanted leadership.

Still, so many people I spoke with said they wanted Obama to be president but feared he could never be elected. Pundits and pollsters dismissed the idea as a long shot at best, self-indulgent at worst. According to some commentators, Clinton even outpolled Obama among black people. By summer, the campaign seemed stalled.

In August, after several grueling months of campaigning, Barack and Michele Obama went to Martha's Vineyard for a vacation with their family and stayed with Valerie Jarrett, a close friend from Chicago. Diane and I joined them for dinner one night, and the five of us sat gazing out at the water on a perfect summer evening, talking lazily. Diane had never met Barack and I had never met Michele, but everyone was so relaxed that we all felt like fast friends.

At that point, I had been asked by most of the Democratic candidates if I would endorse them. I had made no promises, mindful that contested primaries are treacherous waters to swim in. I was grateful to President Clinton for bringing me into his administration in a role I cared so much about. I admired Hillary Clinton. I had also come to know and respect Joe Biden, then the senior senator from Delaware. Nonetheless, I believed that Barack was uniquely qualified to provide inspirational leadership at the national level, and as the evening wound down, I told Barack I would endorse him later in the fall in Boston.

On the way over to the Vineyard, I had talked with Diane about what advice I would give the candidate, and I wrote it down on a scrap of paper. Later, after dinner and dessert and a lot of laughs, it was time to leave, but not quite yet. Still at the dinner table, I told Barack that I wanted to speak to him not as a political tactician, given my limited experience, but as a friend and a citizen about what I wanted to see in a presidential candidate.

"First," I said, checking my scrap of paper, "run like you're willing to lose." I challenged him to say exactly what he thought and believed, because people can read a fake every time and because nothing persuades like conviction. Never mind that some would disagree. Our politics should not require us to agree on everything before we can work together on anything

"Second, run at the grassroots," I said. I was certain that most people resent having self-proclaimed experts tell them what the outcome of the election will be even before they vote. But I also felt, I said, that grassroots campaigning is not simply a political tactic but a philosophy about community. When it comes to politics and civic life, I said, so many feel as if they're on the outside looking in. His opportunity was to go to those who feel left out and invite them in.

Last, I told Obama about the importance of keeping his rhetoric positive and high-minded, that it not only set him apart from other candidates but expressed the kind of visionary leadership the country needed. I warned him of the obvious: Detractors will dismiss what you say as empty rhetoric just because it's inspirational. I shared with him the riff I had developed in my own campaign—"just words"—and invited him to use it if he ever found it helpful. (He did later in the campaign, which produced a minor uproar in the media.)

He listened intently and seriously, with that professorial air he sometimes has. He asked few questions and mostly just nodded. He thanked me warmly. As I started to put my notes away, he took the scrap of paper from me and put it in his own pocket.

As Obama's candidacy came to be taken more seriously, idealism itself was on trial. "Change you can believe in"—one of his most recognized campaign slogans—was an antidote to the naked fear-mongering of his Republican opponents, but his positive message stood out in the Democratic primary as well. During one debate in New Hampshire, Clinton chided Obama for raising what she called "false hopes." This was, for me, one of the saddest moments of the campaign. Why exactly were his hopes false? What made his aspirations inauthentic? Indeed, if they were, we were all wrong about our country's most deeply held values.

Obama, of course, won the Democratic nomination, and just about one year after our quiet dinner on the

Vineyard, I was one of eighty-four thousand people to witness his acceptance speech at Invesco Field in Denver. This vast, modern stadium, built for touchdown passes and bone-crunching sacks, now featured a red, white, and blue stage on the field, adorned with Roman columns puncturing the expanse. The high Colorado sky and warm temperatures made sunglasses and water bottles necessities.

I was both a delegate and a campaign surrogate, so I was asked to arrive well before the evening's formalities began to be available for the press. The national anthem, which officially launched the program, was about to be sung when Jim Braude, from New England Cable News, asked to interview me. Jim was a familiar reporter and I asked him to wait so I could stand, my hand over my heart, and listen to Jennifer Hudson sing. Radiant in a dark short-sleeved dress, she walked onto the blue-carpeted stage, surrounded by the color guard with their rifles and the flags whipping in the breeze. Then she sang with such power and emotion, holding every note like it was her last, while the half-full stadium watched and listened in silence.

I have sung "The Star-Spangled Banner" many times and have heard it many more. At official state events. Before ball games. On television in the quiet of my living room. But now there was a poignancy to the words different from what I had felt before. I knew all about the rockets' red glare and the bombs bursting in air. But there was something new when she sang, "O say, does that star-spangled banner yet wave . . ." She was singing about enduring American ideals.

The flag symbolized a special kind of triumph that day. If only for a moment, some great divide in our country's history closed. Not a racial divide or an economic divide but a human divide. For an instant we reconciled. When she finished singing, I stood back, shut my eyes, and sobbed. All the anguish, all the exasperation, all the frustrated hopes of a generation poured out of me.

Braude was gracious. He left me alone until I gathered myself and was ready to be interviewed. As I walked over to him, I bumped into Cory Booker, the mayor of Newark, New Jersey, and one of the nation's rising black political stars. I asked him how he was doing.

"I'm not going to make it," he said.

"Why?"

"I just fell apart listening to the national anthem."

And both of us burst into tears all over again. By the time I reached Braude, I was laughing and crying at the same time.

Jim's first question of the interview was: "Why are you crying?"

Why indeed.

Later, when Obama took the stage to deliver his acceptance speech, I sat at the back of the Massachusetts delegation and tried to avoid talking to anyone. I just wanted to listen, see, and absorb. Young people, clearly volunteers, were at once stunned and emboldened to realize that they could shape history. Old people, especially elderly blacks, randomly shook their heads, looked off into the distance, or smiled softly. Everyone was transfixed. By the time Obama took the stage, every seat was full—and the roar filled the night sky. The first thing I noticed was the expression on his face: the gravitas, the humility, the realization that this wasn't just a political rally in a Colorado football stadium but a turning point in American history.

We talk about these idealistic American values—freedom, equality, reconciliation—but more often than not they're the stuff we reserve for public holidays or special occasions. After the parades and holiday tributes, we put them back on the shelf and return to the banalities of everyday life. And then this young, charismatic man comes along and invites us to believe in them, and he is a *black* man—someone from a despised quarter of the society—who makes the election not about race but about those very values. After the speech, reporters kept sticking microphones in my face and asking if I felt a new sense of pride because a black man was accepting the Democratic nomination to be president of the United States. That was part of it, no doubt. I felt great pride. But it was the *message*—the tangible hope, the bold idealism—that was the transcendent part for me. That renewal of faith in the possible was what made everything different.

I got a message from an aide that Obama wanted to

see me right after the program. I obliged, but I really didn't want to go. I just wanted to try to take it in, to imprint on my memory the good and wise and proud thing that the people of America had just done and were about to do in November. But I dutifully went backstage after the lights went down and greeted the Obamas as well as Joe and Jill Biden and their families as they came off the stage. I hardly said a word.

Barack had one question: "Was it all right?"

I just nodded.

Obama's landslide election in November confirmed that his message had been heard across the country and that he had lit a spark of idealism for a new generation of Americans. I was elated not only because I felt he would change the direction of the country, but because his victory offered a new template for appealing to voters' better angels.

But I'm not naive. When the tides of cynicism run so deep, change will come slowly. I understand why so many people in our society, young and old, have lost trust in many of our society's core institutions and in the men and women who lead them. The headlines are a drumbeat of betrayal: the greed of Wall Street, the half-truths and outright lies of politicians, the steroid use among professional athletes, the shrill tone of talk radio and cable TV, the tawdry sex scandals too numerous to mention. At some level we have come to expect disappointment and bad examples from prominent people and public institutions.

But defeatism is precisely the wrong message. We need to remind ourselves that, individually and collectively, we can do better. I know that's true, because I see that American ideals are more powerful than any one American who might undermine them. Those ideals were undeniable one summer day in 2008, when I attended the funeral of a soldier.

When I first became governor, I was reluctant to attend the funerals of servicemen and servicewomen from Massachusetts. I certainly wanted to acknowledge their sacrifice and to offer whatever comfort I could to the families, but I worried that my presence would be misinterpreted as grandstanding. My staff urged me to attend, and I'm glad they did. I've tried to be at each one. Though I've been asked to speak, I never do. I listen, I pray, I pay my respects. I simply want the family and loved ones to know that the citizens of Massachusetts recognize and honor the sacrifice that was made for the rest of us—indeed, for American ideals.

What is most striking about these funerals is how young everyone is—the surviving spouse, the boyfriend or girlfriend, the siblings, the friends and classmates. In some cases, the widow cradles an infant son or daughter the dead soldier has never held. Some who gave their lives were immigrants, which is not surprising. About 12 percent of those who serve in the U.S. military are not citizens. Yet they too enlist, serve, and sometimes die in action.

Nelson D. Rodriquez Ramirez was born in Puerto Rico; his family moved to Boston when he was eight and later settled in Revere. Nelson dropped out of high school, moved to New York when he was eighteen, and enlisted in the New York Army National Guard. In June of 2008, he was on his second tour of duty in Afghanistan, on a training mission in Kandahar City with the Second Squadron, 101st Cavalry, when his truck hit an improvised explosive device. Four servicemen were killed, including Ramirez. He was twenty-two.

I attended the funeral at Immaculate Conception Church in Revere, which has served its community since 1888. The church reminded me of many others I have been in—the stained-glass windows, the tower bell, the statue of the Blessed Mother. The mourners' heartbreak was also familiar to anyone who has suffered so deep a tragedy. Ramirez's wife was there, emptied out with grieving, holding firm to their two daughters, one of whom was not yet six months old. The flag-draped casket lay before the altar, attended by an army honor guard. Many of the mourners held American flags. Others wore T-shirts that bore a picture of Nelson in his uniform with an American flag in the background. The image was inscribed with a Spanish phrase, which translates to: "You will live forever in our hearts."

Ramirez's mother, Diana, approached the altar near

the end of the service. "I'm going to say good-bye to my son," she said, and spoke about "Bebo," who loved Six Flags, the Yankees, airplanes, and his precious young daughters.

It was a moving if mostly conventional Catholic funeral mass, but the priest conducted it almost entirely in Spanish. His choice was fitting. The service was for the community, the pews filled with working-class men and women, many wearing jeans or T-shirts. Some were undocumented. Their language was Spanish—some probably spoke no English at all—but this way they could share in the sacrament. It occurred to me that there was no contradiction between their embrace of the Spanish language and their love for America.

When the priest completed the service, he sprinkled the casket with holy water, the end of the mass. Before the recessional, Diana stood and started singing "God Bless America." Soon everyone joined in, more often than not in broken English: no music, just heavily accented words sung from the heart.

Though it was an unspeakably sad occasion, the spontaneous display of patriotism was inspiring. Undocumented in some cases, Spanish-speaking, and working class, surely the bereaved knew how many Americans viewed them— as outsiders, scapegoats, un-American. Yet they betrayed no bitterness and literally embraced the flag, and all that it represents, because they believe in it. They work the jobs that no one wants, they educate their children despite inadequate resources, and they strive for a better life for themselves and their families. Each day they live for American ideals. And on rugged terrain in dangerous, distant lands, they die for them as well.

I've simply seen too much goodness in this country—and have come so far in my own journey—not to believe in those ideals, and my faith in them is sometimes restored under the darkest clouds. I remember one visit to the Holland School in the Dorchester neighborhood of Boston. Dorchester is a bit like the South Side of Chicago of my youth: handsome Victorian homes owned by professionals surrounded by double- and triple-decker flats occupied by the working poor and barely middle class. Today, Dorchester is populated mostly by African Americans and immigrants from the West Indies, the Dominican Republic, and Cape Verde. Living there as well are many Irish holdouts from a generation ago. Small shops sell "ethnic food" (as distinct from how the French cafés and Irish pubs downtown are described), and people get around on the bus and the subway more often than by car. Most of the people work hard and strive to better themselves, but the news is almost always about the gangs and the guns, and my visits there are as often to commiserate as to celebrate.

On one occasion, a young woman who had been visiting her family from out of town had been shot and killed near the Holland School. Shortly after that, an eleven-year-old boy found a .44-caliber pistol in the neighborhood and brought it to school. The community was understandably in an uproar about the violence, so Boston's mayor, Tom Menino, and I went out to the school to meet with the adults, listen to their ideas, and share some of our own.

The meeting was held at the end of the school day. As the children were leaving, heading to their buses or walking home, the parents, neighborhood activists, clergy, and other adults converged on the cafeteria. The contrast was striking. Here were the adults, serious and grim, worry and frustration etched on their faces, trudging toward the school, looking for answers. And here were the kids, playful and curious, sensing from the TV vans with their satellite dishes and extended antennae that something newsworthy was happening.

Before the meeting, I had a minute or two alone in the principal's office to look over my notes and collect my thoughts. I glanced around the walls covered with student art and posters urging academic achievement or healthy choices. After a minute or two, I realized I was being watched. When I looked up, outside the window were a dozen or more little black boys and girls wearing backpacks, beaming and waving excitedly.

It was a touching scene, a reminder, on one level, of how far I've come in my own journey and of how far our nation has come. At their age, growing up in Chicago, I'm not sure I would have recognized the governor of my state, beyond perhaps knowing that he did not have my skin color. But those children, with all their joyful energy and unbridled dreams, reminded me that my work today must be about them, not me. Not the history I am making, but the history they have yet to make.

We each have a responsibility to the next generation. Everyone I have ever known was taught by his or her grandparents that our highest calling is to leave the world better than we found it. Meeting our generational responsibility may involve the grand gesture or a private act of grace or kindness, the historic accomplishment or some more personal form of service to the greater good. But it must be met. And it relies entirely on American idealism.

When I worked in Washington, I noticed that the city is crowded in the spring with tourists, especially schoolchildren on class trips. Seeing them in their T-shirts and sagging pants, speaking their own special slang, asking passersby about the nearest McDonald's, one might wonder where to find the next generation of leaders. But I know they are there. They embrace the lingo and mannerisms of their generation just as each of us has in our own. But some of these children linger for a moment over the inscriptions in the Capitol rotunda or the Lincoln Memorial. Some become quiet when they gaze out across the Mall from the spot where the inaugural address has been delivered for generations. And in that moment of reflection, in that instant of inspiration, lies a seed of idealism waiting to grow.

As long as we do our job, as long as we bear our generational responsibility, those young boys and girls in Dorchester, the students I saw visiting Washington, and young people everywhere will carry with them the very ideals that have shaped the best of this country. And then someday they will lift up their own communities, make their own history, and give the next generation of Americans a reason to believe.

ACKNOWLEDGMENTS

This is not a history book or even a "kiss and tell." It will disappoint those who expected it to be about the rogues and rascals I have met in public or corporate life or who, for the last few years, kept asking if they would be mentioned in it. This instead is a book about the kinds of mostly anonymous, quiet encounters that I have had (and expect we all do) that leave not just a lasting impression, but enduring inspiration. I have more miles ahead in my journey. But for every positive, hopeful, or otherwise useful lesson I have learned, I first thank the people mentioned in this text who have bothered or happened to teach me those lessons.

I met Todd Shuster, my agent, after a lecture I gave at Northeastern University in Boston in the late 1990s. He came backstage afterward to introduce himself and to suggest we get together to discuss writing a book. I did not warm to the idea at first, but I did to him and through many conversations over many years we became friends. He was tireless in his effort to persuade me that I had a story or two worth telling to a broader audience. I am glad he did. More than anyone else, he deserves the credit for collecting some of those stories into this book.

Christine Pride was not the first editor to be assigned this project at Broadway Books, but she was the perfect one. I am humbled beyond measure by the enthusiasm for this project from all the folks at Broadway and throughout Random House, beginning with Steve Rubin and Stacy Creamer. But Christine's personal empathy for the values expressed in this book made the work seem less like work and helped edge me along. And her understanding that my first priority was my "day job" as governor made a huge difference. With her help and fine touch, we finished something worthwhile.

I thank Jim Hirsch, an accomplished and successful author, for talking me through the discipline of writing, for coaxing lots of anecdotes out of me and the friends and family with whom he met, and for giving the text better shape. Todd lent a hand with interviews, too, and Michele Mansilla, my executive assistant and friend of nearly two decades, was indispensably generous in transcribing the interviews in her off time. I thank them all.

So many of the loved ones I write about in this book have passed away. It was thus perhaps a little easier to tell some of the intimate details about their lives and challenges. My wife, Diane, so central to my life and some of the lessons in this book, is to be specially thanked for her willingness to let me tell her story now, while she is still much in the public eye. For that additional reason, she is a remarkable example of strength and courage.

Our daughters, Sarah and Katherine, have had to endure the burden of all children of having their parents tell silly and sometimes embarrassing stories about them to others. However, most children do not have to bear having those stories published in a book. Fortunately, Sarah and Katherine are composed, confident, good-humored young women, and I know they can handle it. My pride in and love for them is boundless. I thank them for their support, consistent honesty, and love.

For those who read this book, I hope above all that they will reflect on and acknowledge the people who have shaped their own best values and given them a reason to believe. Knowingly or not, those are the people who help repair the world.